THE MAGIC WORD

OTHER WORKS OF LUDWIG LEWISOHN

Biography

GOETHE: THE STORY OF A MAN

Autobiography and Philosophy

UPSTREAM
ISRAEL
MID-CHANNEL
THE PERMANENT HORIZON
THE ANSWER

Criticism

THE MODERN DRAMA
THE SPIRIT OF MODERN GERMAN LITERATURE
THE POETS OF MODERN FRANCE
THE DRAMA AND THE STAGE
THE CREATIVE LIFE
CITIES AND MEN
EXPRESSION IN AMERICA
THIRTY-ONE POEMS BY RAINER MARIA RILKE

Fiction

THE BROKEN SNARE
DON JUAN
ROMAN SUMMER
THE CASE OF MR. CRUMP
THE ISLAND WITHIN
STEPHEN ESCOTT (THE VEHEMENT FLAME)
THE LAST DAYS OF SHYLOCK
THE GOLDEN VASE
THE PEOPLE
AN ALTAR IN THE FIELDS
TRUMPET OF JUBILEE
FOREVER WILT THOU LOVE
RENEGADE
BREATHE UPON THESE
ANNIVERSARY

Drama

ADAM: A DRAMATIC HISTORY

THE

MAGIC

WORD

Studies in the Nature of Poetry

LUDWIG LEWISOHN

1 9 5 0

Farrar Straus and Company · New York

ff

PROEM

Jangle the harmony: you trouble
The silken surface of each pool.
Poetry is enchantment: double
Yet one, and thence most beautiful

Because the music and the meaning
Spring from an undivided source.
A poem is an act redeeming
The soul from chaos and from force.

All speech is purest incantation,
Summoning forth the heart of things;
As on the morning of creation
The magic word both says and sings.

PREFATORY NOTE

The chapter on Shakespeare grew out of a brief series of lectures given for the Adult Education Institute at Brandeis University. The chapter on Goethe formed the bicentennial memorial lecture delivered first at Smith College, later before the New England section of the Modern Language Association. A portion of it appeared in the magazine *Tomorrow*. The Homer chapter was written some time ago as the record of an old enchantment. But I would like to emphasize the fact that the three specific studies are based on the theoretical considerations dealt with in the Introduction and the chapter called The Magic Word.

LUDWIG LEWISOHN

Brandeis University
Waltham, Massachusetts
Autumn 1949.

INTRODUCTION

Speculation on the nature of literature began very long ago. It has become a commonplace that Aristotle declared all the arts to be acts of imitation. What is less often remembered is that he described the act of imitation in literature as being effected through rhythm, word, melody, and that he asked of the content of the act to imitate not what *had* happened but what *could* happen according to the laws of probability or necessity. A free but sanely guided creative activity would ask for no better sanction.

There are few more accurate descriptions of literature as it exists than this. As it exists! For it is clear that Aristotle's description does not go behind the given facts. Longinus probed a little deeper in his observation that "thought and style" are "intertwined and mutually enfolded." But his flash of insight remained quite isolated. Critics and poets for many centuries sought merely to justify literature by its uses. Such is the purpose of Cicero's sonorous argument in the defense of the poet Archias; such of Horace's plea for poetry on the ground that the heroes of old dwell in the night of oblivion, *carent quia vate sacro*, because they lacked a sacred bard to commemorate them. In his still useful and im-

mensely influential *Art of Poetry* he came but once to
the edge of a finer perception when he wrote that it is
not enough for poems to be beautiful; *dulcia sunto,* they
must have charm. But these words of his became a mere
tag.

The Renaissance critics and poets leaned heavily on
the Latins. They came, as Sidney said, "to the pitiful defense of poor Poetry" which, in Bacon's words, was to be
justified in its character of "feigned history"—feigned,
that is to say, according to a more hopeful fashion than
that of the dark world of reality. Ben Jonson dwells for
a page on the question of inspiration, of magic, and
quotes the vibrant line of Ovid:

Est deus in nobis, agitante calescimus illo—

"there is a god within us at whose stirring we burn." But
one feels that his own heart remains quite dry. So did
Boileau's, though it became a fashion to say these things,
when he wrote that a man cannot be a poet, "unless he
feels the secret influence of heaven"

S'il ne sent point du ciel l'influence secrète.

Once more in this period we find a soaring moment of
insight as we did in Longinus. It is in Pascal's fragment:
"The meanings receive their dignity from the words"—
"les sens reçoivent des paroles leur dignité." And once
more, as in Longinus, the moment remains isolated, although, amusingly enough, Pascal adds: "Must look
up examples."

They were great centuries of criticism, the seventeenth and eighteenth, from Dryden through Johnson, but only criticism of substance and techniques, of divided matter and manner, never of the ultimate. No one dreamed that there was a secret to be sought or to be uttered. A vague notion that Aristotle counceled the mere imitation of nature prevailed—Nature, capitalized, which, as Pope asserted in a brilliantly written but silly passage, is

At once the source, and end, and test of Art.

He sank even lower when he wrote: "Expression is the dress of thought." On certain levels this notion of the divisibility of literature, of poetry, into two mechanical units, still prevails and has, in fact, been asserted to be true by quite contemporary translators of foreign poetry of the first order.

Illumination could have been expected from the Romantics. But we are not helped by Wordsworth telling us that poetry is the "spontaneous overflow of powerful feeling," and once again a moment of genuine insight on Shelley's part—"poetry is connate with the origin of man"—has no intelligible aftermath. Goethe went far deeper. Indirectly he struck at the root of the matter in his untiring reiteration of the symbolical character of the concrete, in his insistence that all earthly things were in their own nature metaphorical. It remained for the remote and fragile spirit of Novalis to approach the final secret: "Every word is a word of incantation," and

"linguistics is the dynamism of the realm of the spirit."
But no one heard or understood; it is doubtful whether
he quite understood his own remarks, for he drifted on
into metaphysical subtleties.

Our contemporaries have done better. Forgetting for
the moment his own theory of letters, of artistic creation,
as an act of the conscious will, Paul Valéry penetratingly
defined poetry as "a singular, an improbable relation between a sensible form and a significant value," and the
Abbé Henri Brémont, the briefly famous defender of
"pure poetry," was at least on the edge of a profound
cognition when he declared that all the arts aspire ultimately to become prayer again. Rilke went a step farther
when he wrote to a friend concerning his "determination
. . . to regard art not as a selection from the world but
as the total transmutation of the world into magnificence." He wrote *"ins Herrliche,"* into magnificence, but
he meant, doubtless, the transcendent and divine. He
thus came upon the process of art's redemption of the
world to meaning through the magic word. But of the
word itself he had nothing to say.

Is it not strange, since words are the material of human expression, its very substance and texture, the stuff
of which it is made, that no one apparently has sought
the secret of the character of literature in *them,* in the
nature of language itself and as such? Is this not all the
stranger, seeing that words sustain a wholly different relationship to literature, spoken or written, from that sus-
tained by color to painting, by tones to music, by clay or

marble to sculpture? For a streak of color, an isolated tone, a handful of clay have no self-subsistence or meaning of their own, and become meaningful and rhythmic only in the artist's arrangement of them. But words are in themselves and prior to the poet's use of them cry and summons, grief and aspiration, ecstasy and despair, life and death.

No attempt is made in the following pages to penetrate a primal mystery. That would be as impious as it would be foolish. What is attempted is to situate the problem of poetry, of literature, at the ultimate places of its being—word and myth.

THE MAGIC WORD

THE MAGIC WORD

[I]

In that book which is called "In the Beginning" but which is known to the Western world as "Genesis," there is a description of the origin of language, which has seemed strange and perhaps even childish to those generations who were determined to impose the developmental pattern upon all things between earth and heaven. Today, twenty-five years after Whitehead declared music and mathematics to be "original creations of the human spirit," we have recovered our speculative freedom and may join Paul Valéry in suspecting that "the idea of evolution is only a tempting and fruitful notion of the human mind, more exactly representative of that mind's taste for continuity than it is of nature." To music and mathematics language may now be added as one of the "original creations of the human spirit." Under this aspect the verse in Genesis reassumes its sublime significance.

The passage (II, 19) is difficult to translate with precision. There are overtones of meaning in it and the grammatical structure defines and delimits the meaning closely. "Out of the earth"—the *adamah* from which Adam, the human being, had been molded—the "Lord God formed every beast of the field and every bird of

the heavens and brought (each) to the human being to
see what he would call (or cry) out to it, and all that
(whatever) the human being called (or cried) out to it,
to (each) living soul, such was its name." The Lord God,
it will be seen, was passive according to the story. Man
named all things. His naming of them completed and defined creation. Or, rather, it was a second creation or, at
least, a lending of significance to what had been created;
it was also that giving of dominion to man over nature
which had been promised.

Language as the free creation of man, springing from
him full-formed, was a sharp stumbling block to the
scientific materialists and developmentalists. Commonly
they preserved silence on the entire subject. They simply
refused to face the facts; they invalidated their entire
cosmological scheme by failing to retain the evidence on
this point. Erudite philologists sought to help them out
and framed theory after theory concerning the origin of
language, its early stages, its primitive use and function.
The latest of them,* immensely learned and astute, re-
jects all former theories categorically, and frames one of
his own: that man's earliest utterance was the cry (*An-
ruf*) or the call (*Zuruf*) and that hence the first form of
language was the imperative of verbs. But this is, like all
former theories, a purely speculative one. It is an hy-
pothesis with no empiric facts to fit or to explain. For
there exists no such thing as a "primitive" language in

* Dr. G. Révész. *Ursprung und Vorgeschichte der Sprache* (Bern,
1946).

the sense of the developmentalists—a language analogous to a simpler organism from which a more compli-
cated one could be thought to have arisen.

On this immensely crucial point, too, there has been a
vast and half-concerted silence to which, a little to their
shame, even the anthropologists have consented. Rarely
have the hard facts been formulated as clearly as Schopenhauer's intellectual spitefulness impelled him to do:
"It is known that languages are, especially grammatic-
ally, perfect in proportion to their age and deteriorate
progressively. This gradual degradation is a serious argument against that theory of our bland optimists concerning the steady progress of mankind toward better things."
He was probably thinking of Sanskrit and Greek; he
may not even have known that his statement, properly
delimited, is accurate when applied to the languages of
all those primitive peoples who survive or whose speech
survives: the Eskimo, the Bantu idiom of the upper
Zambeze, the Samoan, the countless Melanesian and
Amerindian languages. The speech of all these "savages"
is intricately subtle; grammatical devices bear witness
to the most delicate perceptual and conceptual differentiations. The Syubiya Bantu idiom divides all phenomena into seventeen categories—organic and in-
organic, individual and nonindividual, character and
function, outer and inner. Nouns take prefixes, differing
for subject and predicate nouns, announcing the cate-
gory of the thing they name. Analogous to these seventeen nominal prefixes are seventeen forms of the per-

sonal subject pronoun and seventeen forms of the personal predicate pronoun, seventeen forms of demonstrative, interrogative, indefinite pronouns.* In Samoan, which emphasizes the stems of words, there exist such fine distinctions as exclusive and inclusive dual and plural forms; Eskimos, whose numeral system ends with 20, have five conjugations, and reasonable ease of expression in their agglutinative language requires a vocabulary of 10,000 words.† These instances could be indefinitely multiplied. Nor is there anywhere among these primitive peoples any evidence of simpler archaic speech forms. On the contrary, languages tend to become simpler and inflectional variety to be abraded by long use among great masses of men.

These linguistic facts have long been known; they have been wholly neglected by the scientists and thinkers who have in recent decades sought to impose their view of the nature of the sum of things. Another, far simpler and even more staggering observation has not even been made. It is agreed that there is but one human race in the biological sense. All men are anatomically and physiologically, that is to say, structurally and functionally, identical. The speech organs of Indic and European man, of Chinese and Semite, of Zulu and South Sea Islander, of the Tatar of the Asian steppe and the Amerindian of the Northern plain and the Andean mountains are indistinguishably alike. Yet the permutations of the

---

* F. N. Fink. *Die Haupttypen des Sprachbaus* (Leipzig, 1936).
† *Op. Cit.*

limited number of sounds which such a being as man can utter are unimaginably great in number and variety. Not each separate clan, but each separate and originating speech group, created with the identical speech organs its own inimitable expression which differs in basic psychological approach and phonetic character from every other form of human speech. Why did the Bantus see and express the universe under the aspect of categories? Why did the Semites ground their speech upon tri-consonatal radicals and then supply variations of meaning by vocalization—as though *silk* and *sleek* and *sulk* and *slack* were all variant meanings of a radical *slk*? Why did the Osmanli Turks require for their expression an harmonious system of vocalization, so that dark vowels in the stem (a, o, u,) must take a dark vowel in the plural ending and a light vowel (e, i and the *umlaut*-modified dark vowels) a light?

Once more: these instances could be indefinitely multiplied. America alone furnishes many speech groups of great subtlety and variety and the huge Indic peninsula is a gigantic laboratory of both Aryan and non-Aryan tongues. There are immemorial language islands, such as the Basque in Pyrenean France and Spain, for which no affinities have ever been found; nor have any bridges toward a common origin been built between speech groups as close to each other geographically in historic time as the Indo-European and the Semitic on the one hand, or the Indo-European and the Finno-Ugrian—the tongues of the Finns, Esthonians, Hungarians, Turks—

on the other. Biologically man is one. Language bears witness to his infinite variety as a spiritual being. Each kind or family of man freely created its own kind of speech which expresses its own variety of psychical structure and its own unique reaction to nature, man and God. In the vast welter of human speech there are few morphological analogies; there are few synonyms and the names of basic concepts in the kindred tongues of neighboring peoples—*love, Liebe, amour; spirit, Geist, ésprit*—contain in their subtle but unmistakable shadings the whole character and the whole culture history of the folk who have created and who use them.

These undisputed and indisputable facts: the intricacy of primitive languages and the staggering variety of the forms of human speech re-establish the passage from Genesis as the eternal and universally valid symbol of fact and truth. The concept of man prior to speech is meaningless. Without speech man was not; without the names of things and actions he could not think about them nor make those primordial differentiations between things and actions and their qualities which are abundant in the most archaic and the most primitive languages. Speech *was* the instrumentality by which man attempted to grasp the meaning of his life and of the world. He has worshipped an unknown God; never a nameless one. Man and speech came simultaneously into being. Hence it becomes meaningless to distinguish between language as expression and language as communication or to ascribe priority to either function. Language, like poetry, was both at once and simultaneously.

Within the texture of speech there is found an evident awareness of its character. The soul is the breath of life and the breath of life is language. The Greek *pneuma,* the Latin *spiritus,* the Hebrew *ruakh* and *neshamah,* the German *Geist,* all the names of the soul are the names of the expelled breath of speech. The other Latin words for mind and soul, *animus, anima,* from which so many words are derived in English and in the Romance tongues, go back to an Indo-European stem *an,* the meaning of which is to breathe. That breath of life, which God breathed into the nostrils of man and thus made him into a living soul (Genesis II, 7), is identical with the created word by which man named and controlled and helped to shape his world.

[II]

Having established the fact that language wholly escapes the pattern of developmental theories and that all known groups of men, though biologically identical, created their languages according to the incomparable varieties of the human spirit, let us turn our attention to the constant interior character of speech. We meet at once the both obvious and astonishing fact that language is, as we now say of certain kinds of painting, non-objective. It does not describe; it does not delineate. Words have no discoverable connection with things. It may be, as Plato thought, that words are symbolical expressions of "essences"; it may be, in the elaboration of this insight by Wundt, that words are the gestures of the organs of speech that express the impression things made on man. The fact remains that language is pure symbol. Imitation of nature, when it does occur, is rare or late or in jest. We do not in fact call the dog bow-wow but *dog*, which is the cognate of the German *Dogge*, hound, and *hound*, in turn, is the cognate of the German *Hund*. The Greeks called the animal *kuon* and the Latins *canis* and the Hebrews *kelev*. There is no relation between the word and the object it names. It has been fancifully suggested that man, rounding his lips in imitation of the round shield of the full moon called the satellite *moon*, as in English or *Mond* as in German. But *moon* and *Mond* are, in fact, distant cognates of the Latin *mensis*, month, so that the Germanic peoples seem to have measured time by the phases of the moon, whereas to peoples dwelling under the clearer Mediterranean skies the brilliancy of the moon was more striking than its phases, so that *luna*, the Latin name, is connected with *lux*, light. And farther East and South the Hebrews called the moon *levanah*, the white or radiant one. So men did not call the other heavenly bodies shiners or twinklers but called a star *star* in both English and Sanskrit and *astēr* in Greek and *stella* in Latin and *kokhab* in Hebrew and *kakkabû* in Assyrian. But when the Hebrews looked upon the greater groups of stars or constellations they called them stars no longer but *mazeloth,* the fates or fortunes, wondering not about the physical constitution of the universe but about its relation to man and to man's destiny.

It was in the dark that men looked upon the moon and stars and this darkness divided from the day the Greeks called *nux* and the Latins *nox,* from which come the words in the Romance languages and which goes back to an antique Indo-European stem *nokt–.* And once more the neighboring Semites had an entirely different vocable for our *night* and the German *Nacht.* They called the dark *la'ylah* in Hebrew and *lilatû* in Assyrian, whence we have the fabled name of Lilith, the sorceress, the nocturnal one. A closer connection between words and objects, a realistic connection, might have been expected in the names of ultimate, primordial things and relations. But what correspondence is there between a girl-child and the Greek *thugatēr* which is almost the same in Sanskrit and obviously akin to English *daughter* and German *Tochter?* Furthermore we find men belonging to the same speech groups not using this kind of word at all but the feminine form of the word for son. Thus son is *filius* in Latin and daughter *filia* and hence the Romance languages, like French (*fils, fille*) have all kept this nomenclature. And the Hebrews with an entirely different type of speech form had the same notion, calling son *ben* and daughter *bath.*

A very learned student of language could adduce further examples from a thousand tongues old and new, living and obsolete, languages of primitive groups and of highly civilized ones, and prove over and over again that the names of things have no relation to the things and are, therefore, not picture but symbol, not imitation but creation, not science but poetry, not description but evocation and magic. Yet these examples have all been confined to substantives, to the names of things. Far subtler symbolizations are used in language so soon as we approach the simplest verbal forms and the pronominal forms of substitution for the names of things, so soon as we say in English *he was* and in Latin *fuit* and in Hebrew *hu hayah* or when we regard the simplest possessive pronouns and say *our father* and *pater noster* and compare the Hebrew form *avinu* where the possessive pronoun *nu* is an enclitic, that is, an inseparable suffix. Equally subtle are the names of qualities, the adjectives, and *dear* is *lieb* in German and *carus* in Latin and *khabib* in Hebrew. The simplest conjunction is, of course, an inextricable mystery of intellectual symbolization and varies even within the same speech group, so that we say *and* (German *und*) but the Goths said *yakh* and the Greeks *kai* and the Latins *et* and the Semites *v'*. The briefest reflection will show that genetic considerations in the ordinary sense are useless here; we are faced by the quite ultimate human phenomenon which withdraws itself from any attempt at intellectual analysis. Language is evocation, magic, a pure operation of the human spirit. It is not strange that we find among intense mystics the doctrine of "divine language as the substance of reality" and speculation concerning "a language which expresses the pure thought of God." *

Poets, like mystics, have had their own awareness, at least in action, of the miracle and magic of the word. The contemporary poet's categorical "a poem must not mean but be" overshoots the necessary mark of such a being as man in such a world as the present. For poems have always both *been* and *meant;* they have always been incantatory as well as redemptive or self-redemptive; they have always incarnated both music and meaning, both the cry and call of Adam and the breath of God which made him a living soul. An exact insight into the character of language as in itself symbol, music, magic, would have eliminated many futile controversies and analyses of an unreal object. Once grasped, it renders self-evident the priority as well as the primacy of form, since language itself is symbolical form. But precisely as human speech conveys meaning through the freely created magic of symbolic form, so does poetry; so does, in fact, all literature. Therefore, though he assigned not quite the right reasons, Paul Valéry was supremely right when he declared: "Form is everything . . . a writer who has given his work effective form has founded it on man's constant nature, on the . . . essence of being." So much has, in one way or another, been said before. In his matchless analysis of the ultimate intimacies of the productive process he went

* Gershom G. Sholem. *Major Trends in Jewish Mysticism* (rev. ed.; Schocken Books, Inc., New York, 1946).

further and revealed facts half known but never clearly admitted before: "Substance (*le fond*) no longer causes form, but is one of its effects . . . I am not far from believing that certain profound thoughts owe their origin to the presence or the imminence of that presence in the mind of linguistic forms, of certain empty verbal figures and of a certain tone which evoke a given content."

In this memorable passage there are two errors. Valéry thought that Mallarmé had invented the symbolical character of form and language; he merely emphasized that character anew. Secondly, there are no "empty verbal forms," seeing that words are themselves pregnant with both celestial and earthly fire. Strike poetry at any point! It is never less than meaning; it is always more. Music and magic are the more and other of the poet's meaning; the meaning is the crystallization of the music and the magic. When Vergil wrote *"suadentque cadentia sidera somnos"* he stated a fact, namely, that nightfall brought on sleep, but he stated it in terms of the mysterious universe and of the music of the freely creative word. None of the four words he uses has any realistic connection with the process or thing it names. Each is already a poem about the process or the thing. The juxtaposition of the words with the triple alliteration and the internal rime in their musical order of fall and rise and rise and fall, is intricate yet single as an act. Layers or strata of symbols are within it; the free symbolism of the original words, of their phonetic pattern of alliteration and internal rime, of their rhyth-

mic or strictly musical order. The incantatory quality
is constituted of all these elements. Poetry, as again
Valéry pointed out, consists of a series of such acts,
whose character is wholly alien to nature and belongs
wholly to the spirit of man.

Strike poetry at any point! Pure incantation is found
in such a verse as Catullus' galliambic:

Dea magna, dea Cybelle, dea domina Dindymi.

But how easily might Shakespeare have written and
even so substituted—and at what distance—art for nature: Stain red the waters of the ocean. Actually we
know he wrote:

The multitudinous seas incarnadine

heaping evocation on evocation, symbol on symbol, per-
forming an act as utterly torn out of the context of mere
nature as the most intricate mathematical formula. Such
great magic and evocatory acts occur on every page in
Milton:

Sabaean odours from the spicy shore
Of Araby the blest,

or

Imparadised in one another's arms.

The odes of Keats are great continuous examples. But
poets of the second rank, like Matthew Arnold who
thought, amusingly enough, that the magic of poetry
had something to do with the Celtic spirit, strike out the
intense magic word in

The unplumm'd salt estranging sea

or

Lone Daunis and the high Cephissian vale.

The magic of nomenclature is not the purest. It has adventitious aids. Quite pure in its effortless blending of limpidness and evocatory power is—to choose at random from a thousand instances—Goethe's

Hab doch auch im sonnenhellen
Land gelebt, geliebt.

It is the sonant magic word that leaves Victor Hugo a great poet when we have allowed for the thinness of his meanings:

Oh! quel farouche bruit font dans la crépuscule
Les chênes qu'on abat pour le bucher d'Hercule!

What is known as "modern" poetry, the kind that may be said to have arisen (roughly speaking) with Stéphane Mallarmé and the French symbolists, differs from the poetry of the past merely in the heightened consciousness of the poets of the character of the word and of their art. When Mallarmé wrote *"la blancheur sanglotante des lys,"* he used the word *sanglotante* with a new awareness of the magic, nonconceptual character of language. He emphasized the magic element consciously. He sought to repeat the act of Adam and cry out to a thing the new name of a quality. He inaugurated the free use of linguistic magic, music, symbolism —that free use, consciously escaping the rein of logical

pattern, which has doubtless led to some singularly triumphant acts of creative beauty. It was this deliberate
escape from the conscious patterns of logic that enabled
Rilke to write:

> Und alles ist wie ohne Alter:
> die Landschaft, wie ein Vers im Psalter,
> ist Ernst und Wucht und Ewigkeit;

it was this free use of the magic word that permitted
Valéry to compose his enchanting verses:

> . . . et certaines
> Moins captives des rythme et des harpes lointaines,
> S'en vont d'un pas subtil au lac enseveli
> Boire des lis l'eau frêle ou dort le pur oubli.

There are no examples of this "pure" and "difficult"
poetry in the English language to match either Rilke or
Valéry. It had not matured prior to the two World
Wars. The poets who wrote in English were, for the
most part, afflicted by an anachronistic scientific ma-
terialism which never touched the mystic Rilke and
which the engineer Valéry saw through and transcended. Among Americans, the angry repudiation of
their country, which set in with Ezra Pound—their tragic
alienation, their spiritual homelessness in both the world
and the universe—produced the opaque and tortured
and helplessly cacophonous work of the neo-esthetes
from Wallace Stevens to, let us say, Delmore Schwartz.
They did not, like Rilke or Valéry, produce plastic and
musical creations whose latent meanings will shine

more and more through the density of a manifestly and immediately difficult texture. They blankly despaired of any meaning; often they dared not utter the residual meanings in them. One of them alone, or almost alone, was from the beginning so luminous with wit and charm and music that he did not mumble unbeautiful obscurities but spoke out with the gesture of an angelic dead-end kid. That was, of course, e. e. cummings, who summed up the matter for all his colleagues:

> We doctors know
> a hopeless case if—listen: there's a hell
> of a good universe next door; let's go.

What is clear from all this, however, is at least the fact that all the work of these writers could not have come to be, had not a sense of the free creative character of language rearisen, of language as expressive gesture, magic, incantation, divorced from the direct representation of both thoughts and things.

[III]

Poems have always, to return to the variant of Archibald MacLeish's line, both been and meant. The magic of the word was, on one level, to have literally a magical effect. From most great literatures these folk forms are lost. The Song of Deborah, the earliest document in Scripture, is stylistically as intricate, as highly wrought as Milton. We happen to have fragments of archaic

Latin, far later in time than the Song of Deborah, which
are simple incantatory hymnal cries to the gods, charms
chanted by the Arval brotherhood, individual magic
formulae against, for instance, the gout. And so early in
Latium people sang

> Divom templa cante
> divom dea supplicate

and knew, as the verse shows, that there were present
both music (*cante*, sing thou!) and meaning (*suppli-
cate*, pray thou to the god . . .) and that the music
of the song was inseparable from the rhythmic pattern of the words. And an afflicted individual chants:
"I remind thee to cure my feet. Hold the pest in the
earth, keep health here in my feet."

> Ego tui memini
> medere meis pedibus:
> terra pestem teneto,
> salus hic maneto
> in meis pedibus.

Here we have poetry, literature, reduced to its simplest
form: the freely created, symbolic rhythmic word; inevitably rhythmic according to the phases of the heavens and the motions of the body in breathing and in
love is meant to cure, to heal. It is meant to redeem. It
is to do so by man's identification of himself with some
numen, some divine power, which is the *thou* of the incantation. And here we come upon the inner nature of
the meanings of poetry, of creative literature. These are

almost never didactic; they are inherent in the creative functioning of the word which was not to man primarily a means of communication but of expression and redemption. The redemptive identification with some god or *numen* rose even in earliest ages to identification with heroes or saviors, more man than man himself, representative, redemptive symbols; it became finally identification with the poet, the creative speaker who grasps by mythopoeic power the totality of things and who does indeed, from Homer to Thomas Mann, summon forth by the magic word whole worlds—meaningful and redemptive visions—that never were and that are nevertheless more real than any earthly things and freer than are those from the storms of circumstances and the tooth of time.

Now literature is undoubtedly still both magic and magic formula. The artist who utters the word or formula is first eased or cured of his own ill or pain, and by communicating the magic formula brings vicarious cure and purgation of spirit to his hearers. But literature does not consist wholly of the lyrical forms—poem, personal essay, confession. The larger and more widely persuasive form of creative speech has been and has remained the story, the myth—the story which, whether dramatic or narrative in form, has always striven to be myth and breaks down, as the novel is breaking down today, when that striving is in vain.

What is myth? To him who creates myth, whether dreamer or seer of an earlier world or poet or novelist

of today, it is a story by means of which he seeks to
body forth for himself and his fellow-men all that he
knows, all that he believes concerning life and love and
death, concerning man and God. It is a meaningful
story. It is a story that utters or implies both speculation and faith. Or, putting it differently, it can be said
that man has always projected his deepest beliefs in the
form of stories, of fables in which acting and suffering
men and women were involved because all the great
meanings of life are inherent in the stuff of which stories
are made. Myth is everything and anything except what
the Concise Oxford Dictionary calls it: "a purely fic-
titious narrative." It is a story in which matter and
meaning are identical, a story which incarnates a vision
of the sum of things, a story which, though it deals with
the concrete, means to communicate the universal and
eternal.

A close study of even a few great masterpieces,
Oedipus Rex, the *Divine Comedy, Hamlet, Faust,* would
have made this point clear enough. It is, however, one
of the highest distinctions of Freud and his disciples to
have revealed the concrete mythopoeic faculty as active
in contemporary man. Dreams, like myths, are neither
fortuitous nor meaningless. The dreamer speaks through
his dreams. But he speaks poetically; he speaks by
metaphor and symbol. He does so partly because this is
his way of speaking at all, language itself, as has been
seen, being metaphor and symbol, and partly because
ethical inhibitions and social taboos keep him from ut-

tering directly certain repressed but indestructible desires. Thus what Freud called the manifest content of a dream is a tissue of symbols and substitutions. It is a little personal myth precisely like the myths we find in legend and in fairy lore. The latent content—the thing the dreamer sought to *say*—must be interpreted from the symbols used in the little myth.

Gradually it was discovered that all dreamers use certain common symbols in order to say in that veiled fashion things that are broadly common to human nature. Finally it was seen that these symbols are in many instances the same symbols which men in the mythopoeic ages used in their legends, in their myths, in their tales of beasts and men and heroes and gods. And since, moreover, it is certain that the neurotic patients, whose dreams were analyzed, flee from the demands and intricacies of life into an earlier world of reverie and dream, there is nothing anomalous in the circumstance that the interpretation of myth and legend, of folklore and, in the end, of literature, too, was derived from the analysis of people who had somehow lost their way in the world. As Thomas Mann declared in a memorable context: "The ultimate depths of the human soul are also the primordial depth of time." Dreaming and waking we today use the very techniques by which the antique fathers of the race created myth and lore and legend. Science and philosophy themselves derive from those magic formulae by which primordial souls sought to master the strange universe; all creative literature derives from the myths which were, always and at once, religion and poetry, faith and song, meaning and music, and to that mythic character all great and permanent literature tends in all ages to return.

How could it not be so? For myths, like dreams, are true not because they conform to outer fact but because they express the realities of the soul. Man made myths in his soul's image and believed them because he had made them thus. Therefore they were and have remained far truer to the essence of human life than stories merely invented by later men. This accounts for the well-known fact that the greatest artists from the Attic dramatists to Shakespeare and Milton, to Racine and Goethe, to Wagner and Thomas Mann, almost never invented their fables but used mythic and legendary material already deeply rooted in the consciousness both of their peoples and of mankind. Through these they expressed themselves to their fellows. Through these they could speak both for themselves and for all men. Immensely individualized as personalities themselves, they thus returned to that core of man's life at which myth and faith, shaped by man's essence, wrought in the image of his eternal self, are indissolubly one.

Most modern writers have struggled with so much anguish to achieve works so much more meager and so transitory because they were stranded, as it were, upon a bleak and empty shore. There were no longer either heroes or gods; great myth was reduced, until the other day, to empty fable. All ages but this were dark and ignorant. Faith and form were outmoded; the great game of equating man, the whole man, that fugitive from nature, with his biological make-up, set in. So the modern writer had no significant substance ready to his hand and had to wring substance from observation and personal experience. Instead of using his creative personality as the shaping principle of form and specific meaning, he had to make that personality itself both source and substance of his work. He had to try to be himself god, hero, priest and sacrifice, and to turn his own narrow life and experience into representative story, acceptable myth, into speech that would speak not only for himself but for all men. The lamentable results are all about us. The initial élan of the communication of personal experience and observation is stone dead. Each novel is a drearier or more contorted specimen of an exhausted mood and impulse. The unredeemed masses will inevitably mythologize not Thomas Mann but Taylor Caldwell. Poetry has withdrawn into a realm of sterile mumbling since, as Mark Van Doren said recently, even "music in words is suspect." We are in a desperate twilight region—a desert of melancholy muttering, unpierced by a single cry of man's heart, a single utterance of music or of aspiration.

It is this melancholy situation which justifies or, rather, renders imperative, an act of both scrutiny and recollection. When we turn our eyes once more upon man's real character and that of his expression we remember, undeterred by the materialist fool, that human language is a free and poetic creation by which this human being, torn out of the order of nature, knowing good and evil, stranded inscrutably upon this planet in the depth of space, spoke from the first of the mystery of himself and his being and cried out for his God. He created significant myth in rhythmic measures. Having done so, he achieved varying degrees of redemption from darkness and from guilt. In brief, he started, long before letters were invented, the composition of what was to be called literature. And literature will last as long as he himself lasts unchanged in character and purpose.

HOMER

[I]

At the beginning of Western literature stand two names of incomparable magnitude and meaning: Homer and Moses. At the foundations of every civilized mind there stand no less these two. Until the leprosy of mechanistic barbarism crept upon us there was no well-conditioned child in all the Western world who did not begin his imaginative life with the Creation and the Tower of Babel, with the patriarchs and with the epic of the Exodus, and who did not next know and remember forever the two stories that deal with the wrath of Achilles and the wanderings of Odysseus. Through many ages Homer and Moses and the works ascribed to them were the cornerstones of culture, of a humane life, of a true sharing of civilization, and poets and painters and sculptors and composers filled the world with works drawn from these two ultimate sources of inspiration and served in turn to keep those sources themselves free flowing in the minds of men.

Throughout that long span of time no one or hardly anyone doubted the existence of the mighty poet or the mighty prophet or their authorship of the works that bore their names. Close students could not but be aware of superficial discrepancies in the texts that had come down. In Homer, for instance, there are passages of moral sentiment far nobler and so perhaps of far later origin than the life and sentiments delineated in the poems themselves. His language is not only an archaic Ionic Greek which in this form was never spoken by any group of men, but contains inexplicable vocables of pre-Greek origin. Sensible men explained these matters to themselves as best they could. But when the modern science of philology, useful and even precious on its own strict ground, was invented, there occurred a revolution of attitude which bedevils and afflicts us still. In dusty studies men with dusty minds, wholly ignorant of the nature of the poetic and mythopoeic imagination, took to pieces the great creative texts and treated them as a spiteful cross-examiner in a petty court might treat a poet dragged in to bear witness to some concrete and dreary incident. They found that the witness was not wholly consistent; he dared to shift his point of view; he dared to take two attitudes to the same matter; he used different locutions at different times. "Aha," they said, "you did not witness the incident after all. You were not there. You are an imposter. You do not even exist. The evidence shows . . ."

The great game of textual criticism for the elimination of anyone who knew more than a textual critic began in the case of Homer with the publication of the *Prolegomena* to Homer by Friedrich August Wolf in 1795. Wolf maintained that the ultimate origin of the *Iliad* and the *Odyssey* is to be found in oral tradition which, rightly interpreted, is not only correct but was a brilliant piece of inference for his time. But he maintained in addition—and it is this argument that has done so much direct and indirect harm—that the extant texts of the poems are of multiple authorship. For Homer, for the divine and immortal poet, he substituted a crowd of astute scribes and redactors, even as his fellow countrymen in the next century substituted for the divine and immortal prophet to whom we owe the Pentateuch in *this* eternally significant form a "Jahvist" called J. and an "Elohist" called E. and an author of a priestly codex called P.

It happens that when Wolf's *Prolegomena* to Homer appeared one of the world's great poets was among the first readers of the essay. And this poet, Johann Wolfgang Goethe, wrote to his friend and fellow poet Schiller under date of May 17, 1775, as follows: "I have read Wolf's Preface to the Iliad; it is interesting enough but profited me very little. The idea may be well enough and the effort deserves respect. The trouble is that gentlemen of this type in order to cover their weak flanks will occasionally lay waste the most fertile gardens in the realm of beauty and turn them into wretched fortified trenches. And in the end there is a stronger subjective element than one might think in all this trash."

Thus the last word on this sorry matter was spoken at once. The philologist fails to apprehend the creative act as such and turns its results into stuff not above the capacity of a glorified philologist. And in that itch to

reduce all things to his level instead of revering that
which is higher than himself, in that desire to fit all
great things into the narrow compass of his uncreative
and prosaic mind lies that strong "subjective element"
on which Goethe put his unerring hand. This disease of
reduction to a common level of the great phenomena of
life and history and literature has spread and still afflicts
the half-educated. Whenever the so-called Homeric
question has been approached by a man of true poetic
temper it has in that narrow and spiteful form simply
vanished. The late Andrew Lang, one of the most ac-
complished students and translators of Homer in the
world, a learned folklorist and ethnologist in addition,
summed up the question one hundred years after Wolf
first raised it.

> The dust and awful treasures of the dead
> Has learning scattered wide, but vainly thee
> Homer, she meteth with her Lesbian lead,
> And strives to rend thy songs; too blind to see
> The crown that burns on thine immortal head
> Of indivisible supremacy.

What are the facts? Was there a poet named Homer
who sometime in the ninth century B.C.E. made up the
Iliad and *Odyssey* out of his own mind? The fundamental answer is this: no poet makes up anything out of
his own mind, whether he write epic or drama or novel.
The poet's mind gives form and meaning, significant
form, to the meaningless welter of existing fact and
event; the poet's mind is the fire that burns clean of

dross and hardens into form the given substance—that substance which has come to be in modern life often only the poet's experience and observation but which in the great mythic ages of literature even as late as Shakespeare, included the history and the myth of whole peoples and all the songs and all the ballads of the folk singers of that people as raw material for the fusing fire of the great poet's creative act. Wherever we have great and integrated form and style and vision, as we have in the *Iliad* and the *Odyssey*, we know that we are face to face with a personality—*one* personality—whose creative act gave rise to that integrated form and style and vision. And there is no reason why in view of the universal voice and testimony of all antiquity we should not call him Homeros, Homer. He himself is legendary. True. There are no materials for a biography in the modern sense. Seven cities, according to the old scholastic hexameter, contended for the glory of having given him birth:

Smyrna, Chios, Cholophon, Salamis, Rhodos, Argos, Athenai.

But the reason for that is not at all the reason which an average philologist or even a biographer like M. André Maurois would suppose. In the great mythic creative ages, earlier or later, the artist thought not of himself but of his work. He thought of his work as lending immortality not to himself, as the modern writer does, but to something beyond himself. The anonymous architect of the Cathedral of Chartres thought of the glory of

God. Homer thought of the Greeks and Trojans and of
that lamentable war and of gods and heroes. And since
he lived somewhat before the Greeks had learned the
art of writing from the Semites, he must himself have
first said or sung his poems to pupils or disciples in the
art of epic poetry who remembered them, as men de-
monstrably do and can before the day of the written
word. And so his personality as such in an age when
men honored others by mythologizing them and not by
"debunking" them faded into the mere symbol and
metaphor of the poet—*the* poet of all the Hellenes,
whose poems were recited at stated times and intervals
as part of the public life of the Greek people and formed
the foundation of the education of children and youths
as long as Greece was Greece.

It was no accident that this was so. For in the
Homeric poems the Greeks saw that glorified vision of
their heroic age which they themselves had helped to
create in the image of their souls and their souls' temper, and which was consequently not only true *to* them
and *for* them but far truer than any drier chronicle of
demonstrable fact could have been. Like the Hebrews
who had first to conquer Cana'an, or the Angles and
Saxons who had first to conquer the land they were to
call Angle-land or England, the Hellenes or Greeks were
not indigenous to that land in which they were to become a people and which, as the Jews did Cana'an and
the Saxons England, they were to make their own and
render illustrious forever. It was apparently around the

turn of the second millennium before the Common Era that those kindred tribes whom Homer is fond of calling Achaeans or Argives or Danaans began to conquer and to colonize Greece and the Grecian isles and the opposite Asian shore.

If now the historians and the archaeologists are right in placing that war against the city and citadel of Troy around the year 1200 B.C.E., then the historical foundations of the Homeric tales were laid in a period some centuries after the Hellenic conquest but not long enough to obliterate its memories or legends. It is certain enough from both tradition and analogy that these first conquering and then settling clans and tribes had bards and singers who celebrated gods and commemorated the heroes and heroic deeds of their ancestors. These bards sang baladesque poems and passed them on to their disciples; they developed, however crudely, the hexameter in which from Homer on all the epical poems of antiquity were composed. And finally, between roughly 850 and 830 B.C.E. nearly four centuries after the Trojan War, came Homer, who knew all the ballads of all the ballad-makers and all the stories told by hearthfires and in market places and who forged and fused all that he had heard and learned into the two great poems that bear his name.*

---

* The analogous process took place in our own age when, in 1849, Elias Lönnrot published the Finnish epic *Kalevala* which he wrought into a stylistic whole from songs and ballads taken down from the lips of the folk minstrels of Finland. Cf. Martin Buber, *Die Rede, die Lehre und das Lied* (Leipzig, 1917).

Though a great personality and therefore a great stylist, Homer conceived of himself both literally and poetically as belonging to that guild or order of bards and singers who had from earliest times accompanied the Hellenic clans. This process of imaginative identification with predecessors, with the admired and beloved of old, is a constant factor in human biography and especially in the biography of creative spirits. Many acts and attitudes of the artist have in the past and are even in the present dictated by a mythic tradition within which, whether always consciously or not, he conceives of himself as living and working. To his own immortality he desires, as it were, to add the immortality of the poet as such; he wants to range the heroes whom he celebrates in that order or class of heroes whom other poets have added to the permanent memories of mankind. Thus Milton was uplifted and consoled by thinking of

> Those other two equalled with me in fate,
> So were I equalled with them in renown,
> Blind Thamyris and blind Maeonides,
> And Tiresias and Phineas, prophets old.

Thus some quite contemporary poet or novelist in this dusty, turbulent and yet pedestrian twentieth century will secretly identify himself with other, older, mightier exemplars of the creative spirit and so

> claim consort with the great and strong
> Who suffered ill and had the gift to speak.

· 33 ·

Nothing convinces us more of Homer than his own delineation of the poet and minstrel. Of such delineations there are two, both in the *Odyssey*. There is the minstrel-poet Phemios in Ithaca; there is Demodokos at the court of King Alkinoos of Phaeacia. Both were attached to the kings or chieftains; both were held in the highest honor. Telemachus, the son of the wandering Odysseus, returns against his will to the banqueting of his mother's suitors who are consuming his inheritance.

Unto the suitors sang the illustrious minstrel; in silence
Sate they and gave ear. He chanted the heavy home-faring
Destined by Pallas Athena from Troy unto the Achaians.
To the storey above resounded the heavenly singing
Heard by Ikarios' daughter, the pensive Penelopeia,
Swiftly did she descend the lofty stairs of her dwelling . . .

Tears in her eyes she turned to the divine minstrel:

Phemios, many and other enchanting stories thou knowest
Surely of men and gods, that are current among the minstrels.
Chant then one of these to the men about thee—in silence
Let each drink his wine. But from that lay, the most grievous,
Do thou desist. For ever it rends the heart in my bosom,
Since upon me, above all, the ineffable sorrow descended.

But Telemachus defends the minstrel against even so mild a remonstrance.

Mother, why blamest thou the precious singer, for that he
Seeks to delight us with songs that in his soul have arisen.
Blame belongs not to him, the minstrel. To Zeus, to Zeus only,

Who at his whim and pleasure apportions the woes of us
   mortals.
Blame thou the minstrel not, though the Danaans' woes are
   his story;
Ever it is the newest lay that above any other
Gains the loudest applause of every attentive assembly.

In spite of the antique romantic setting—the banqueting hall, the singer with his lyre—the whole scene
has a not unmodern or, rather, a permanent note and
aspect. Homer wants to show us that at least in the heroic age which he is describing the minstrel was one of
the most honored of men, that he was and ought to be
free to sing as he chose, Fate alone being answerable
for things as they were, and that he should, if he liked,
choose the most contemporary of subjects in order to
command the attention of men.

An even nobler figure than Phemios of Ithaca is that
other minstrel-poet Demodokos whom Homer shows at
the court of Phaeacia—that sea-washed, sun-set realm,
fabulous and exquisite, withdrawn into a strange golden
age even within the framework of Homeric form. Here
Odysseus was cast alone upon the shore; here he was
found by the king's daughter Nausikaa and her maidens;
here in the high and gleaming hall of Alkinoos he re-
counted the tale of his mythic adventures. The banquet
was prepared. The king summoned the princes and
nobles to honor the mysterious stranger. He cried:

Summon the god-like minstrel!
Call Demodokos, him whom the god has richly inspired

With the grace of song which his heart commands him to
    utter.

And so the banquet was prepared.

Now appeared the herald, leading in the minstrel belovèd,
To whom, though dear to the Muse, both good and ill she
    has given,
Quenching his eyes but bestowing on him the sweetness of
    music.
For him a silver-studded chair the herald brought forward,
Placed it among the guests beside the loftiest column;
Next he hung on a nail the resonant harp at the minstrel's
Head, and guided his hands so that he could reach it.

They washed their hands.

When the desire for food and drink was thoroughly sated
Bade the Muse the minstrel the praise of heroes to utter.
From the lay whose fame in those days climbed even unto
    heaven
Chose he the quarrel of Odysseus and Achilles, the scion of
    Peleus.

Neither singer nor king nor guests knew that the stranger whom they were honoring according to the laws of
hospitality was Odysseus.

Thereof sang the famous Demodokos, the while Odysseus
Grasped with sinewy hands the purple mantle that swathed
    him,
Drawing it over his head, his noble countenance hiding,
Lest the Phaeacians behold the tears that were staining his
    lashes.

But whenever the god-like minstrel paused in his singing,
Swiftly he dried his tears and from his head drew the mantle,
Grasped the double beaker and poured to the gods a libation.

Alkinoos, seeing the emotion of his guest, proposes those gymnastic and warlike games and contests so dear to the Greeks of all ages.

But we see and hear Demodokos once again. Before Odysseus departs for his homeland, Alkinoos prepares in his honor another of those Homeric banquets of roast meat and wine which have been the vicarious delight of the ages. And again Homer places the poet at the center of the action.

Now the herald approached and led in the minstrel, the
    precious,
Honored of men on earth, Demodokos; and he bestowed him
In the midst of the hall, near a lofty pillar to lean on.
Him, the herald, summoned the much-experienced Odysseus,
Carved the succulent saddle—yet kept the share of the lion—
Of the white-toothed swine, in bloom-fair fatness embedded:
Herald, give thou his share to Demodokos that he may eat it.
Though my heart be sad yet would I do him a kindness.
Do not all mortal men on earth take heed of the minstrel,
Giving him honor and reverence due, since none less than
    the Muses
Teach him the lofty strain in love of the race of the minstrels?

When everyone's desire for meat and drink was satisfied the much-experienced Odysseus turned to Demodokos:

Truly above all men, Demodokos, thee do I honor
Zeus's daughter, the Muse, or Apollo himself was thy teacher.

For thou chantest the fate Achaian so strictly, so truly,
As though thou hadst been there and hadst heard and experi-
   enced and seen it
Oh, sing on, sing on . . .

Demodokos does the bidding of Odysseus. He sings
that tale of high and strange exploit. And so, Homer
tells us, "Odysseus melted in melancholy; tears bedewed
his eyelashes and cheeks." And then follows one of
those great and intimately and immortally human si-
militudes of Homer which, like the description of the
poet and of the poetic process point, even though cast
into a mold become traditional, to the feeling heart, to
the seeing eye of a man—*one* man who knew, like his
great imitator Vergil, the tears of mortal things. Odysseus wept

Even as weeps a woman and throws herself on her dear
   husband
Who in combat fell defending his town and his people
Seeking to turn the bitter day from his home and his chil-
   dren;
Seeing him quivering there in the terrible death-throes
Wildly doth she embrace him and ululates, while the fell
   foe-men
Wildly strike with a lance upon her back and her shoulders,
Bind her and drag her away as a slave of toil and of sorrow
Into pitiful exile where wither her cheeks once so blooming:
Thus to arouse compassion tears poured from the eyes of
   Odysseus.

It is true beyond doubt that the Homeric poems existed for ages only orally. There is no reason why we
should distrust the witness of all antiquity that a text—
not quite ours—was reduced to writing under Peisis-
tratus of Athens around the year 600 B.C.E. Other texts,
proceeding from other sources of oral tradition doubtless existed side by side with the Peisistratean text. And
hence in the second century B.C.E., Aristarchus, the li-
brarian of the great library of Alexandria, undertook to
establish an authoritative text of Homer, even as several
generations of critics undertook to establish an authoritative text of Shakespeare. The *Iliad* and the *Odyssey*
which we have may not be in every line the poems that
Homer sang; we are not sure that the Shakespearean
plays are in every line conformable to the forever lost
manuscripts of the poet. But we know the two poets;
we know them by the two unmistakable marks of creative personality—by vision and by style, by form which
is personality.

[II]

Wherein lies the poetic supremacy of Homer?
Wherein lies his undying interest? Why do both men
and boys (women significantly rather less!) read him
today in an hundred tongues unheard of and unborn
when he gathered the legends and the lays of his people
and remolded them into enduring form? There is the
sheer story interest, no doubt, ruder and more barbaric

in the *Iliad*, as befits a tale of primitive rape and re-
venge and warfare, lovelier and softer and finally tragic
in a nobler sense in that other tale of the home-faring of
Odysseus and the waiting of the faithful Penelope and
the reconquest of his home and hearth and little island
kingdom by the much-suffering, much-experiencing
hero. But it is easy enough to imagine such tales told in
rude balladesque style and with a murky or limited
vision or with less freshness of feeling and less deep and
exquisite humanity. And there are in truth such tales in
the Nordic epics and ballads which are read dutifully
enough by scholars and students and philologically
trained patriots. The plots are not inferior to those of
Homer. But there is not the Homeric world; there is not
the Homeric feeling and style; there is not, as the old
phrase has it, that sense, despite sadness and barbaric
misery, of the morning of the world.

Civilization could not have been young when Homer
lived and created. Indeed we know that it was already
old. We know that great empires had already risen and
fallen and upon their ruins others had already risen and
fallen in Egypt, in Asia, in Crete. Yet Homer makes us
feel as though the world were fresh and dewy from the
hand of God, and as though men had just learned the
arts and crafts of life and rejoiced in the beauty of
things and in the simplest exercise of their skill and
were, though mature and tragic enough and conscious
of death, newcomers upon dawn and sunset and wheat
and the sea and the earth and themselves. We mark this

extraordinary quality first perhaps in those recurrent
epithets of the Homeric style. Horses are "beautifully-
hooved" and the oars and the tables and the bathtubs
are "beautifully-smoothed" and harmony among men is
"heart-refreshing," whereas disharmony is "heart-de-
vouring," and words are "winged" and the earth is
"many-nourishing" or "food-giving" and the sea—one
has a vision of the unchanged Mediterranean billows—
is the "far-uproaring" and women are "white-elbowed"
and "beautifully-braided" and the ships are "vaulted"
and the chariots "fair-wheeled" and the wild boar of
the crags and the hills is the "sow-mounting boar."
These epithets may be traditional, as scholars have supposed, and a part of the epic style of the minstrels who
came before Homer. But whether that is true (and the
evidence is of the slightest) or whether this is Homer's
personal style (with whatever hints from his predecessors), the effect upon the reader of all ages has been
magical and is so still. For what that reader feels is that
the swathings of use and custom and weariness and reiteration have suddenly been taken away from the
world and the things that fill it, and that he is brought
once more into direct and immediate touch with those
qualities of nature and artifact which are beauty—
beauty itself.

That freshness of perception and closeness to things
and innocence of vision make Homer's style immortally
delightful. One may proceed from the famous epithets
to single lines or couplets:

Thus spake she and bound to her feet the beautiful sandals,

or

And the sun sank down and darkness covered the pathways,

or

Sweetly twanged the string and bright as the voice of the
swallow,

or

Gently the West wind breathed o'er the roaring billows of
wine-red,

or

And these were the daughters of springs and of groves that
give shadow
And of the sacred streams that pour themselves into the ocean,

or

Even as in a garden the poppies bend their heads sidewise
Heavy with their own fruit and with the rain of the spring-
time.

The world is luminous and translucent both. All things
are beautiful in their own nature. Nothing needs to be
done or to be considered to make them so. The tragic
doings of man—and these, as we shall see, Homer views
quite starkly and without illusion—cannot touch the
beauty and delight of nature or of man's stamping upon
nature the image of his skill and need. Such is the inner

structure of those famous similes which arise so effort-
lessly from scenes of darkness and cruelty.

> Like the poplar
> Which grew tall and straight in the deepest glade of the
>   marshes
> Smooth of stem, at the summit alone were branches with
>   foliage,
> And which the wainwright fells with the gleaming edge of
>   his iron,
> That he bend it wreath-like to be the wheel of a chariot;
> Weathering lies the fallen tree on the shore of the river—
> Thus lay Anthemion, Simoeisios' son, when his armor
> Ajax, the hero, robbed.

The poet is quite sovereign here. Neither Anthemion
the slain nor Ajax the slayer dreamed of the image of the
felled poplar prone in the marshes. It is the poet who is
aware of the larger world and the deeper connections;
it is he who, at least at moments, rises above the web of
illusion and enmity and cruelty and mere desirousness
in which men live entangled. The beauty of nature and
of the eternal processes and the beauty and goodness of
the peaceful occupations of man are always parts of the
poet's immediate cognition with which he tempers and
with which he enlarges the evil, bitter and barbaric
matters that he has to relate. This objectivity and de-
tachment on the part of the poet and this delineation
of human action and passion against the background of
the eternal and beautiful world—these are the two elements that make up the narrative technique of Homer.

And it may be said that this technique is still incomparable, that all other great narrators, whether in verse or prose, have learned it and that no narrator has ever entirely neglected it except to the hurt of himself and the permanent interest of the tale he had to tell.

The world of Homer is luminous and fresh and entire. Man in spite of his inner darkness feels that too. And he expresses that feeling through the joy in his skill and in the qualities of the material of the natural world. Thence arise the famous and fascinating descriptions of the sceptre of Agamemnon and the shield of Ajax and of the gifts offered by Agamemnon when he hoped to conciliate Achilles, and the royal garments donned by Agamemnon and the helmet of Odysseus and of the objects which Telemachus found in the treasure chamber of his father and of the house of Alkinoos in Phaeacia and of the chair of Penelope, well-wrought and inlaid with ivory and silver, a work of art. Let us regard closely one of those descriptions and let us choose the somewhat less familiar one of Helena as Telemachus sees her when he visits Lacedaemon to ask Menelaos for news concerning his lost and far-faring father.

While he revolved such thoughts within his sense and his
    spirit
Helena floated in from her lofty and odorous chamber
Like in form to Artemis, her of the golden-wrought spindle.
Now a dainty chair for the queen Adraste brought forward,
And at her feet Alkippe spread the soft wool of the carpet.
Phylo fetched the basket of silver, Alkandre aforetime

Gave it to Helena, she, the wife of Theban Polybos,
Dwellers in Egypt were they in palaces loaded with treasures.
Menelaos in turn gave her two ewers of silver,
Tripods twain as well and gold in the weight of ten talents.
Other beautiful gifts to Helena gave the Egyptian,
Gave her a spindle of gold and a spinning-basket of silver
Which was wheeled and rolled and gold surrounded its edges.
Phylo now, the industrious maid, did set it before her
Filled with yarn in balls and on the yarn was reposing
Wound with wool of violet hue the golden-wrought spindle.

This is, of course, one of the more sumptuous Odyssean passages and points to a very archaic period in which the Greeks borrowed heavily of the civilization of Egypt. But precisely for that reason it illustrates well the wonder at works of skill and beauty as well as their rarity and also the simple and elemental uses to which they were put. Helena appears in the hall of her palace with her yarn in a basket like a modern tea table in mechanism, but spins the violet-colored wool on a spindle which, though made of gold, is of the most primitive type. Objects such as these were, of course, rare in the Homeric world; they were as famous as works of art; they became the heirlooms of regal houses. But the point is that for this very reason the joy in them is as fresh and as dewy as the joy in the beauty of nature. Nothing is worn or stale; earth is not cluttered with objects; it is, somehow morning; it is, somehow dawn; even though we know from the age of human civilization that that morning, that that dawn dwelt primarily, dwelt overwhelmingly in the poet's heart. Though the Greek people as a people had created its myths and legends, it was the sensibilities of the poet that edged them with pathos and with charm. Not the rude warriors of the *Iliad* nor the softer characters of the *Odyssey* suffused bloody and cruel tradition with immortal loveliness. It was Homer. It is from Homer that the world learned the legends of his transformed and transfigured world. A dark primitive tale tells of a woman who slew her son and was changed into a nightingale. It is Homer who sings:

As when the nightingale, Pandareos' brown-plumaged
    daughter
In the beginning of spring renews her beautiful singing;
Sitting under the foliage of wide-branched trees and um-
    brageous
Higher and higher and swifter she rolls her melodious
    chanting,
Foolish woman, lamenting her son whom she slew, the be-
    lovèd
Itylus, son of King Zethos.

It is from these lines that the poets of the world drew their inspiration. Across the ages echoed not the barbaric tale but this transformation of it and found ever new embodiments even to Arnold's magnificent chant: "Hark! ah the nightingale! The tawny-throated!"

Style and vision which together make form—these are the great preservatives. The excellence of any work of the human imagination is the excellence of its form

in this ultimate and deeper sense. And so the supremacy
of the Homeric poems is also to be explained by the
supremacy of their form. Rude barbaric warriors drowse
by their fires awaiting another day of slaughter. It is
the poet who sees and says:

Numerous as the stars on a cloudless night and refulgent
So shone forth, in front of Troy, by the bed of Xanthus
Between that and the ships, the Trojans' numerous fires.
In the plain there were kindled a thousand fires; by each one
There sat fifty men, in the ruddy light of the fire:
By their chariots stood the steeds and champed the white
    barley
While their masters sat by the fire and waited for morning.

[III]

Let us now examine the world which is forever new
and fresh and significant in Homer's form. For that
world has come through the ages to be more than a
poetic world. It is, rightly and necessarily, the permanent symbol of the European pagan world and its ethos
and temper, close enough to the East—to the world of
Moses, to the world of Amos and Isaiah—not unallied to
that East in certain superficial ways and manners yet
wholly untouched by it. The Homeric people are in
some sort Orientals themselves. They have nothing of
the supposed "Aryan" stoicism and serenity. Men as a
mark of respect kiss the shoulder of a superior, as is still

done in the Near East. In grief they bear themselves like all the other East Mediterranean peoples:

Wailing they sate themselves in the dust and plucked out their head-hair.

They weep copiously and unashamedly, as Aeneas was later to do in Vergil's poem. When Odysseus longs for his homeland we see him thus:

Shedding tears he gazed far out o'er the waste of the waters.

When he reaches that land

Kissed and embraced he that land while scalding tears poured down gushing
Over his cheeks.

And when at last he and his son Telemachus recognize each other Homer says:

And there arose in both a sweet desire for lamenting.
Louder they wept than weep the birds and keener their wailing
Than of hook-beaked vultures and eagles from whom some farmer
Took their young ere these were fledged to fly in the open—
Thus to move pity these two wept tears of mighty emotion.

No, they are not impassive "Aryans," these people of Homer. But of the troubled conscience and God seeking of that East which was so near to them they have no trace. Their gods are simply human beings who are strong, immortal, beautiful and above all law. It is this gigantic arbitrary humanness of the Homeric gods that makes the tales of their loves and intrigues so fresh and telling, because these tales are merely tales of men liberated from troubling limitations and so apt for the satisfaction of those reveries in which men dream themselves freed of duty, compassion and law. In the non-human or superhuman aspects of the gods, the aspect of their identification in some sort with rule and fate, we have the first expression of the deep pagan pessimism of Homer and his world.

Thus did weave the gods the fate of pitiful mortals,
Destined to dread and woe, while they however are care-
   free.

And the highest of the gods in his highest aspect is still a tyrant without a heart:

Father Zeus, thou art surely the cruellest of the immortals!
Pity hast thou none for the creatures thou hast begotten,
But condemnest them all to live in need and in sorrow.

Pessimism in its metaphysical aspect of a blind and un-caring universe can go no farther. And so we find indeed that the people of Homer have no very high opinion of man and his life:

Like to the leaves of the forest even so are man's generations:
These the wind doth scatter abroad, but others already
Sprout in the budding woods when comes the spring of
   renewal—
Thus with man's generations: one grows, the other doth
   perish.

This deep pagan pessimism has sounded down the ages nowhere more strikingly than in the famous speech of Sarpedon to his comrade as they prepare to storm that wall which the Greeks had built about their ships:

Dearest one, if we could, if once we escaped from this battle,
Bloom forevermore, unageing no less than immortal,
Nor I myself would take my place in the ranks of the fore-
    most
Nor would I urge thee on to engage in man-honoring battle.
But since a thousandfold the fates of death do surround us
Which no mortal has ever escaped or ever avoided,
Let us win glory of triumph ourselves or give it to others.

Here we have the consent to war, tumult, murder rationalized on the pagan principle of the essential worthlessness of human life. And that principle can be said to be mitigated but little by the belief of the people of Homer in that world of shades in which still float and waver the ghosts, "weak-headed" and forgetful with their Lethean forgetfulness, of those who once were men and women. Memorable is that scene of Odysseus faring to the underworld. He gives the shades blood to drink and for a moment they remember and speak. And the words of Achilles, famous as those of Sarpedon and quoted and used by poet after poet even to Heine, complete the picture of the pessimism of the Homeric Greeks:

Seek thou not to console me for death, O famous Odysseus!
Rather would I be the serf of an indigent peasant

Living himself in need and plow his fields for a pittance
Than be king and lord of the armies of the departed.

We find that ultimate pessimism in all the works of
the Greeks, of whom the last and latest still find their
temper well and clearly mirrored in the Homeric poems.
Homer is far from being without his moments of ethical
insight, as when he says of men:

For through their own misdeeds did they prepare their
    destruction.

And this moral insight rises to sublime heights in the
Attic dramatists. Nevertheless in him and in them and
in all Greeks down to the latest poets of the Anthology
there lies behind this moral insight the shadow of a profound and fatalistic pessimism. So Homer is most con-
vincing when he says:

    He prepared thy lot and thine the duty to bear it,
or

Unto the earth, fulfilling their fate, sank the sons of Antenor.

Or when he makes the dying Patroclus say to Hector:

It is thy season to boast and thou boastest enough. But thy
    conquest
Comes from Zeus himself and from Phoebus—*they* have
    subdued me
Easily as gods could, themselves disarming my shoulders.

It is that same ultimate pessimism that we hear in
Aischylos:

Seeing bravest, best and wisest
But the plaything of a day,
Which a shadow can trip over
And a breath can puff away.

We find its highest expression in the incomparable epilogue of Sophocles to King Oedipus:

                     Now by Fate
To such a depth precipitated down
As not a wretch but may commiserate.
Beholding which and counselled by the wise
That Nemesis regards with jealous eyes
Man's overmuch and at his elbow stands
To shake the full cup in the steadiest hands,
Deem not the wisest of tomorrow sure,
Nor fortunate account him till he dies.

It prevails through all the Hellenic centuries, that fatalistic pessimism, and meets us last in a late and anonymous contributor to that Anthology of Greek poems which John Lascaris saved from the ruins of Constantinople when the Saracens destroyed the city and which he caused to be printed in Florence in 1492:

The circling sun and moon indeed are fair:
The rest is pain and fear and discontent;
And if some little joy to man be sent,
Yet must he surely in return await
A nemesis, a joy-avenging fate.

It is the steady prevalence of that dark fatalism through the centuries which is so significant for the

whole development of Western civilization and literature. In Homer himself it seems to fit the subject, the
manners, the character and the events. For though he
sought to inject into the world he was delineating the
higher perceptions of his far later day, that world was in
its own nature one of imitigable barbarism. The note of
that world is sounded by the wise old Nestor, most revered of the Greeks:

Let us continue the slaying of men! Then may ye all calmly
Strip on the field and plunder the corpses of them ye have
slaughtered.

This being the aim, courage and bodily strength and
agility are the ideal qualities.

Courage Zeus gave thee not, the greatest power among
mankind.

And in a more generalized fashion:

For no greater fame adorns the life of a mortal
Than which strength of hand can gain him or swiftness of
shank-bone.

Nor is this unnatural within the Homeric context. The
fighting is all hand to hand. Individual combats of leading heroes decide a battle. Armor, weapon and garment
being precious and rare, the victor strips the victim and
hurries off with his booty. The bodies of the slain are
left for the dogs and vultures to devour. So much Homer
accepts from his point of view as natural and proper.
Nor is he disturbed when Diomedes butchers the sleep-

ing Thracians. But here and there the even darker
savagery of an earlier age comes through. Achilles sac-
rifices twelve Trojan youths on the funeral pyre of
Patroclus, though everywhere else in the poems human
sacrifice is absent. One has a constant suspicion that the
body of Hector was not only dishonored and stripped
but mutilated. Other primordial customs appear in ves-
tige in, for instance, the marriage of the six sons to the
six daughters of Aeolos, King of Phaeacia. Finally at the
end of the softer and more human Odyssey, primitive
human torture is described both implicitly and ex-
plicitly. It is only hinted that the disloyal maidservants
were tortured before they were hanged. No conceal-
ment is practiced in regard to the fate of the false goat-
herd Melantheus:

Off they sliced his nose and ears with the edge of the iron,
Tore his phallus out as food for the dogs of the household,
Cracked the bones of his hands and feet.

Therewith, Homer calmly remarks, "the work was completed." Odysseus goes through his house with a pan of
burning sulphur to fumigate it against the stench of
death.

Nor is this all. The Homeric heroes are shrill brag-
garts and gossips; they scold like vulgar shrews: they
are morose and self-regarding on the lowest plane;
kindly or chivalric feelings are rare among them and
must be wrung from them by appeals to their vanity
and their fears of fate. Yet aside from the tragic fact

that European man has not much changed in these respects and still delights in torture and war and bragging of his superiority, even the civilized and sensitive reader accepts somehow the barbaric men of Homer, partly because the whole world in which they lived is suffused by the beauty and freshness of the Homeric perceptions and sensibilities, but also because side by side with the murder and clamor and torture there is in Homer a deep and exquisite humanity, a humanity unrivaled in certain aspects in all literature.

That humanity expresses itself primarily in an appreciation of domestic love, of the family, of the relations of husband to wife and wife to husband, and children to parents. Of romantic love or falling in love there is hardly a shadow in Homer. Sex is enjoyment like wine.

Both of them entered the room of the grotto, the beautiful vaulted,
And partook of love and rested next to each other.

The man in this case was Odysseus. But this partaking of love had no relation in his mind to his intense desire for home and hearth and wife. It is the marriage bond and relation which in Homer creates the best values of human life:

For there is nothing better nor to be desired upon earth here
Than when man and wife in heartfelt affection united
Tranquilly rule their house.

He is moved by marital or parental love even in the animal world:

As when a bird to his naked young their nourishment
  bringeth
Careless though he himself be beset right sorely by hunger.

He remembers the lovely gestures of children in the
midst of a battle scene;

Back he stepped like a child that nestles close to its mother.

He draws his tenderest similes from home and hearth:

Joyful as unto children the healing of their dear father.

He generalizes and allies these sanctities with men's native earth:

For there is nothing sweeter than our own homeland and
  parents
Even though afar from them amid alien people
One possess a splendid house afar from the loved ones.

He is realistic enough concerning the characters of men,
but also concerning those of women:

Thou knowest the mind of a woman!
Ever she seeks alone to enrich her immediate bedfellow,
Giving thought no more to her children or to the husband
Plighted to her in youth.

And there is the substance of a comedy in the one line
in which we are told why Laertes, the father of Odysseus, never approached the once beautiful Eurykleia:

Never he touched her at all in fear of the rage of his lady.

But these sardonic touches are rare. They are offset by a
deep tenderness for woman, high or humble, as she

faithfully performs the simple tasks of life. A moment of stalemate between the Argive and Trojan hosts reminds him of that:

> the hosts stood
> Even as the balance when an honest wife spinning for wages
> Weighs the wool with faithful scale exactly adjusted,
> Thus to earn a scanty wage for the bread of her children.

And through the ages has shone the nameless figure of that poor serving-maid whom Odysseus hears in the watches of the night as he hopes on the coming day to slay the suitors of Penelope and be reunited to his wife and kingdom. Twelve miller girls, we are told, ground on handmills each night the wheat flour and the barley flour for the bread of the suitors' ruinous banquets. Eleven of them had gone to rest. Only this poor girl was awake.

She kept grinding on for of all of them she was the weakest.

At last she quits her mill and prays to Zeus to destroy the suitors

> Who through the soul-sickening work of grinding the flour forever
> Make my knees to give way. For the last time let them go gorging!

Odysseus accepts as omen and happy prophecy the poor girl's words as Zeus affirmatively thunders above the heads of king and bondmaiden.

It is no wonder then that at the center of both the

Iliad and the *Odyssey* stands a married pair, the beauty of whose love and faith tempers the often intense savagery of the actions and passions described in the poems. The origin of the chief Homeric action, the war against Troy, is of course in the rape and theft of Helena by Paris, the son of Priam, King of Troy, from her husband Menelaos. But Helen is never entirely human. She has indeed one great moment when from the towers of Troy she beholds the hostile hosts of her countrymen and her words at that moment are among the most celebrated in Homer:

Clearly the rest I behold of the dark-eyed sons of Achaia;
Known to me well are the faces of all; their names I re-
    member;
Two, two only remain whom I see not among the com-
    manders,
Castor fleet in the car, Polydeukes brave with the cestus,
Own dear brethren of mine—one parent loved us as infants.
Are they not here in the host, from the shores of loved
    Lacedaemon,
Or, though they came with the rest in ships that bound
    through the waters,
Dare they not enter the fight or stand in the council of
    heroes,
All for fear of the shame and the taunts my crime has
    awakened?
So said she.—They long since in earth's soft arms were re-
    posing,
There, in their own dear land, their fatherland, Lacedaemon.

Inhuman and allied rather to gods than men as Helena
is almost throughout the poems, it will be noted that she
shares the Homeric tenderness for parents and children
and the home of childhood and that she seeks in no wise
to gild or justify the crime of passion through which she
brought on the ten years' war and the lamentable deaths
of men.

The married pair that we remember from the *Iliad* is
the Trojan prince and his wife; it is Hector and Andromache. And perhaps beyond any scene in all literature
this scene, though barbarous in the context of its events
and necessities, touches and will forever touch the very
heart of the most sacred of human relationships. Hector
in full armor is about to issue forth from the gates of
Troy to fight the Achaeans. On the wall Andromache
and their little son Astyanax meet the husband and
father.

> And behold with a smile the boy regarded the father,
> But at his side appeared Andromache bitterly weeping.

She pleads with Hector to defend the citadel from
within the walls. She recounts to her husband the misfortunes of her own parents which have left her with
none to love or lean upon but him.

> Hector, behold, thou art to me now both father and mother
> Thou art brother dear, O thou my beautiful husband!
> Have compassion on me and stay on the tower of the fortress!
> Make not an orphan thy child, make of thy wife not a widow!

Hector's heart is torn. But pride and the knowledge of the danger of his folk and city bid him fight. So he must go forth even though his prophetic soul tells him that there is no hope.

For that day will come, my soul is assured of its coming,
It will come when sacred Troy shall go down to destruction,
Troy and warlike Priam too and the people of Priam.
And yet not that grief, which then will be, of the Trojans
Moves me so much—not Hecuba's grief, nor Priam my
    father's.
Nor my brethren's many and brave, who then will be lying
In the bloody dust, beneath the feet of their foemen—
As thy grief, when, in tears, some brazen-coated Achaian
Shall transport thee away and the day of thy freedom is
    ended.
Then perhaps thou shalt work at the loom of another in
    Argos,
Or bear pails to the well of Messeis or Hypereia,
Sorely against thy will, by strong Necessity's order.
And some man may say as he looks and sees thy tears falling:
See, the wife of Hector, that great pre-eminent captain
Of the horsemen of Troy, in the day they fought for their city.
So some man will say, and then thy grief will redouble
At thy want of a man like me to save thee from bondage.
But let me be dead and the earth be mounded above me,
Ere I hear thy cries and thy captivity told of.
Thus he spake, the radiant, and stretched out arms to the
    boy-child,
But to the bosom back of his nurse, the beautiful-girdled
Bent the crying child in fear of its own dear father,

Terrified by the steel and the mighty mane of the helmet . . .
Then did laugh the father dear, then laughed the dear
    mother.
And from his head the helmet took the radiant Hector,
Set it shimmering on the ground, and into his arms he
Took his own dear child and kissed and in his arms rocked
    him.

He prays to the gods. He prays that his little son be
some day a greater and a better man than he. He puts
the child into its mother's arms. She presses him to her
fragrant bosom not without tears. Hector, moved to the
very soul, caresses her with his hand:

Yield not, O dear wife, too much to grieving and sorrow!
None can despatch me to death's abode without destiny's
    ruling.
Yet remember that from his fate fled never yet mortal
High or low, from the hour when first he had vision of sun-
    light.

He bids her go to her domestic tasks, ruling and direct-
ing the maids of the household. He must go away to
war. He puts on his helmet with the far-fluttering horse's
mane. She goes, the dear spouse, turning back often toward him amid her tears.

    It is this scene that the heart and mind remember and
that dwells with the reader through the battle and tumult of the *Iliad*. It occurs in the sixth book. And it is
exceedingly strange that less fame has attended the almost equally beautiful and affecting passage at the end
of the twenty-second book when, Hector slain and out-

raged by the brutal Achilles, Priam his father and Hecuba his mother and Andromache his widow bewail his death and their loss. Especially poignant is Andromache's description of the probable future of Astyanax, her fatherless child:

Ah, the day of his father's death robs a child of his play-
 mates;
Ever he lowers his eyes as in shame, a sob shakes his bosom.
Wanting the child goes about among the friends of his
 father,
Tugs in beseeching one by the coat and one by the mantle;
He who takes pity on him will still be penurious in
 giving . . .
Weeping then the child will seek his mother, the widow,
Our Astyanax, think! who once on the knees of his father
Sucked the marrow of bones and with tender lamb's flesh
 was nourished:
And when weary of play and fain for rest would repose him
On the softest weaves or in the arms of his woman
In his lovely bed, his tranquil heart full of sweetness.

Is it surprising that these figures, Hector and Andromache and their child, have lived in the imagination of mankind for eight and twenty centuries? Manners change and customs. But the human heart has not changed at all; neither has in its essentials the art of narrative or of dialogue and Homer is still the first and still the greatest of that long line of creators, from himself to yesterday's novelist, who have sought to interpret the life of man through the significant forms of art.

The *Odyssey*, softer, serener, more ocean-washed and sun-swept than the *Iliad*, has for its entire framework an action and a passion of domestic love. For though Odysseus desires naturally enough to regain his house and little island kingdom of Ithaca and to see again both his father Laertes and his son Telemachus, the central object of his yearning through all his long faring over land and sea is his wife, Penelope. She is indeed, not only by a modern appraisal but by Homer's definite though implicit opinion, the highest and purest of his characters. Though the years drag on and her child grows into a youth and no news comes to her of her husband, and though the other island chiefs beset her sore to remarry and not to wear out her youth and fairness in vain waiting, Penelope remains true and steadfast and not only true and steadfast but tranquil, wise, erect. She guards, so far as she can, her husband's rule and substance; tenderly she cherishes her aged father-in-law; circumspectly she brings up her man-child; she even has her subtleties, but she uses them in the service of her unbroken purpose. Doubtless the legend, long known and long told, furnished Homer with both the story and the characters. But it is not without significance that he has grouped about Penelope or placed in her mouth the highest ethical passages of the poems, of which the content and feeling belonged unmistakably to *his* age and not to that far remoter and almost savage one in which the actions of both poems take place.

Throughout them both we had indeed heard of the

one great virtue of hospitality, pleasing to gods and men. Of a certain warrior early in the *Iliad* it is said:

> Well was he beloved among mankind
> Hospitably receiving all men while he dwelt by the high-
> road.

We also read in the *Iliad* that all those who are strangers or in want are under the special protection of Zeus. Such was evidently the highest moral reach that Homer could find in the old heroic age. In the last books of the *Odyssey*, in spite of the vestiges of raw savagery in the details of Odysseus' vengeance which came to Homer doubtless in legend and tradition, a higher note is struck. Odysseus appears at first in Ithaca and before Penelope in the guise of a poor, aged, much-tried beggarman. Obeying the rules of hospitality, she takes him to her own hearth. She asks him after his name and origin. He evades the question and pleads against such a renewing of his woes as an answer would demand. He speaks of her:

> None, O queen, abides upon earth's immeasurable reaches
> Who speaks blame of thee whose glory soars to heaven's
> fortress
> Even as doth the glory of a king god-fearing and blameless
> Who while he rules a mighty folk of vigorous heroes
> Still guards justice itself. For him dark loam of his kingdom
> Wheat will bear and barley; his trees will be ever in fruitage,
> Fertile will be his cattle, with fish his waters be peopled,
> For that he wisely rules and happiness brings to all mankind.

That great dialogue between the unknown Odysseus
and the wise Penelope goes on and culminates in a
speech of Penelope's in which the poet has expressed
the highest knowledge he had, the highest that a pagan
world reached either in him or in those who came after
him:

Very few are the days that are given on earth to us mortals.
He who thinks without ruth, whose acts are cruel and
  brutal—
All men wish him, the while he lives, but sorrow and ill-luck,
And in death itself his name is an abomination.
But the noble of thought whose actions are equally noble,
His most worthy fame will strangers spread to the far ends
Of the dwellings of men on earth and bless him for goodness.

Needless to say Odysseus, first recognized by his father,
next by the dog Argos, at last by his son, achieves vengeance and victory and is united forever to his faithful
spouse. Nor is there any action in the long roll call of
stories from that day to this in whose issue the natural
heart of man takes a deeper satisfaction.

The natural heart of man! It is that which beats in
Homer. Of the cognitions of the great redeeming
thoughts that have arisen east and west he knows
nothing. But neither upon the whole does the common
run of men under whatever mere name history has destined them to live. To them earth's days are few; of
values beyond themselves they know little or nothing;
life to them is a battle in some sort as is the *Iliad* or it is
also in some sort a journey as is the *Odyssey* and the

very best they know and the source of all their dearest
joys are those sanctities and domestic affections, that
married and parental love with its loyalties and delights
centering in hearth and home, which Homer so incom-
parably depicts and places as the one surely good and
precious thing in the midst of war and tumult and
cruelty and wandering and homelessness and death.
And that fundamental and hitherto constant vision of
human life he has embodied in a form at once so spontaneous and so radiant, so filled and thrilled with all the
voices and appearances of earth and sea and sky, man's
natural habitation and home, so freighted with myth
and legend which, though not intellectually explicable,
are instinctively clear to that ultimate depth of the soul
which is at one with the ultimate past of human history,
that he is still, despite the centuries, the greatest, clear-
est and, strangely enough, most continuously interesting
of poets. That well-known gibe of Horace that even the
good Homer nods at times was morose and sophisti-
cated. Open the two poems of Homer where you will.
He grips you at once. The story carried along by the
roll and surge of the hexameter bears you with it. You
may hate fighting; you may and will think his gods foolish and even hateful. The great art and the great humanity of the first of poets silence all protest. Other
reputations have risen and set; a few have risen again
from dusty centuries. Homer shines through the ages
with an equal brilliance still undimmed.

SHAKESPEARE

[I]

The national poets of great human groups, whether these groups be political or linguistic or both, tend to become sacrosanct. They are no longer men or writers; they are symbols of pride and honor. Their countrymen, even the unlettered ones, identify themselves with the national poet; he can do no wrong; he cannot have written ill. His texts are studied in the schools and though the schoolboy may not have greatly relished epic or drama, the book becomes intertwined with his recollections of boyhood and youth, home and first love. To the schoolmaster, moreover, the works of the national poet become a matter of vested interest; they become so no less to research scholar and historian and antiquary. To justify their work, which often enough loses touch with the values involved, it must be antecedently assumed by these men that the literary values are beyond the reach of cavil, of change of taste and time.

No great national poet has suffered more severely from this process than Shakespeare. The Greeks were luckier in the matter. Even the remote modern, reading him in an alien tongue, can find no fault with Homer. The French, on a quite miniature scale, were lucky too.

Racine is a small poet beside Shakespeare or Homer. But his taste and judgment within his limitations are perfect. He cannot be exalted beyond a certain point, but neither can he be diminished. Utterly different, too, is the case of Goethe. He was a modern; he is ours. Once you relinquish to time those works of his which, but for fragmentary passages, belong to an older world, you feel that the rest, that those works which do survive, are as fresh as this spring's blossoms and as close to our essential business as this morning's news. But Shakespeare comes from a world remote and almost medieval; he and the men of his age could soar and sing; the vast exuberance of a great liberation was in their gestures and their voices. But all was tentative, immature, volcanic. Judgment is precisely what was far to seek in both the writings and the lives of the men of letters in that age. Chaucer was a good writer and Dryden was a good writer in the sense in which, though far above them, Homer and Milton and Goethe were good writers. And in that same sense André Gide and Thomas Mann and George Santayana are good writers among the living. Well, from that point of view, no Elizabethan and almost no Jacobean poet was a good writer. Neither was Shakespeare. His purple patches are the most dazzling ever uttered by mortal lips. Except in a few of the supreme tragedies and one comedy they remain purple patches. His genius was boundless; his judgment was small. He wrote hurriedly and raggedly; the earlier views of him are sounder than those of the romantic nineteenth century, which may be symbolized by Coleridge's speaking of his "aweful name" and insisting that his judgment was equal to his genius. This type of adulation reached its intensest point of self-intoxication in the Shakespearean essays of Swinburne. Since then the tide has receded. But the fact has hardly been consciously marked. It is time that that be done.

What was that older view of Shakespeare which the Romantics despised so heartily and misrepresented so thoroughly? They desired, both the German and the English Romantic critics, to have discovered Shakespeare. Shakespeare needed no discovering. The witnesses to his greatness are the great English men of letters from his familiar friend Ben Jonson through Milton, Dryden, Pope, Johnson, to the very threshold of the romantic movement. If editions of his works were few, it was because readers in that period were also few. But it was during the central years of the English Augustan age, from 1726 to 1734, that the labors of Lewis Theobald first established a sound text. And Theobald was partly impelled to his labors by the fact that the chief of the Augustan poets, Pope, had, as a matter of both gain and glory, edited the works of Shakespeare and had done the editing superficially and ignorantly. Such was Shakespeare's fame in the period most alien from his style and temper.

His glory was contemporary with himself and never truly dimmed. It was first and most memorably as well as most discriminatingly expressed by his friend and

fellow-dramatist Ben Jonson. And Jonson knew both the
man and the poet. One of the few reasonably authenti-
cated anecdotes concerning Shakespeare is that one according to which the occasion, if surely not the cause, of
his final illness was a merry meeting of himself, the poet
Michael Drayton and Ben Jonson at which "he drank
too hard." Now there are two documents by Jonson concerning Shakespeare and if we put the two together we
have a critical judgment both perfect and complete.
First there are those great memorial lines which are familiar to many. "I confess," Jonson wrote,

> thy writings to be such
> As neither man nor muse can praise too much.

Therefore the poet takes, as it were, a deep breath to
utter an adequate eulogy.

> Soul of the age!
> The applause! delight! the wonder of our stage!
> My Shakespeare, rise; . . .

He opposes a plan to exhume the bones of Shakespeare
at Stratford and transfer them to Westminster Abbey on
the ground that Shakespeare needs no tangible memorial:

> Thou art a monument without a tomb.

He compares him not only to the fellow dramatists of
his age, as being above them all, but to the tragic poets
of Attica and Rome, whom Jonson knew well in the
original.

Triumph, my Britain, thou hast one to show
To whom all scenes of Europe homage owe.
He was not of an age, but for all time!
And all the Muses still were in their prime,
When, like Apollo, he came forth to warm
Our ears, or like a Mercury to charm.

In these very lines, by the way, the stylistic uncertainty, the sudden rise and equally sudden fall, of even the most self-conscious craftsman among Shakespeare's contemporaries is eminently clear. But praise can have no greater energy or splendor. There was, however, another side to the matter on which Ben Jonson, a great sitter and talker in taverns, especially to that group of younger poets known as the "sons of Ben," expatiated in private. And this other side, in order to keep the record straight, as we should now say, he recorded and published in his charming prose-fragments called "Discoveries Made Upon Men and Matter." Here Jonson wrote: "I remember the players have often mentioned it as an honor to Shakespeare that in his writing, whatsoever he penned, he never blotted out a line. My answer hath been 'Would he had blotted a thousand!' Which they thought a malevolent speech. I had not told posterity this but for *their* ignorance, who chose that circumstance to commend their friend by wherein he most faulted . . . he flowed with that facility that sometime it was necessary he should be stopped. . . . His wit was in his own power; would the rule of it had been so too. . . . But he redeemed his vices with his virtues. There was ever more in him to be praised than to be pardoned." Hardly more need be said. Nor did Dryden say more in his succinct and splendid summing up. "I cannot say he is everywhere alike; were he so, I should do him injury to compare him with the greatest of mankind. He is many times flat, insipid; his comic wit degenerates into clenches, his serious swelling into bombast. But he is always great when some great occasion is presented to him; no man can say he ever had a fit subject for his wit, and did not then raise himself as high above the rest of poets—"*Quantum lenta solent inter viburna cupressi.*"

Nor did Voltaire, whom the Romantic critics could not be expected to love, go farther. He complained, in fact, that no one had hitherto "translated any of those striking passages which make up for all his faults." He made Shakespeare, as Paul Valéry justly observed, a European figure; he spoke of that "genius full of energy and fecundity, of nature and sublimity, without the least spark of good taste." Bound to his age, his final tag about the supposed Aristotelian unities may be overlooked.

Johnson, when his observations are closely looked upon, did not go quite as far as his predecessors. Being twitted by Garrick with being a heretic in respect of Shakespeare, he replied: "I will stand by the lines I have written on Shakespeare in my prologue at the opening of your theatre." These lines, now half-forgotten, are worth quoting:

When Learning's triumph o'er her barbarous foes
First rear'd the stage, immortal Shakespeare rose;
Each change of many-coloured life he drew,
Exhausted worlds and then imagined new:
Existence saw him spurn her bounded reign,
And panting Time toiled after him in vain.
His powerful strokes presiding truth impressed,
And unresisted passion stormed the breast.

We live in a darker and a soberer age than did the nineteenth-century Romantics. Our temper is nearer in certain respects to that of Johnson than to that of Coleridge. To us, too, it seems as though Shakespeare was the first to emerge from a barbarous age, that his exuberant and untempered genius often spurned the bounded reign of existence and that it is true of himself and of many of his characters that a too unresisted passion stormed their breast.

Now it is a curious fact that this older view of Shakespeare which does not so much diminish his glory as serve to define it, harmonizes far better than the nineteenth-century apotheosis with the little that we know and the very little more that we dare infer concerning Shakespeare the man, the human being, and as *such* the author of these poems and these plays.

[II]

The most authentic personal word we have concerning Shakespeare is again a word of Ben Jonson. It is the word "gentle," which he uses twice, both in the lines on the portrait and in the celebrated memorial verses. "My gentle Shakespeare!" In harmony with that epithet is also the now long hackneyed invocation as "Sweet Swan of Avon!" No one would have chosen such words to characterize Marlowe the man or Ben Jonson himself. The word remained. Immediate tradition crystallized it. A very few years after Shakespeare's death, in full possession of such reminiscent talk as follows the eminent dead, Milton wrote in "L'Allegro":

> Then to the well-trod stage anon,
> If Jonson's learned sock be on,
> Or sweetest Shakespeare, Fancy's child,
> Warble his native wood-notes wild.

These were, like all the words of Milton, weighty and well-considered. No highly wrought and perfect work, like those of antiquity, had come from the hand of the gentle English poet, but "native wood-notes wild," the swift products of dazzling genius in which, as Milton had earlier written

> to the shame of slow-endeavoring art
> Thy easy numbers flow—

and from which, as his friends and colleagues, the players, had assured Ben Jonson, "he never blotted out a line." How, indeed, could he have done so who wrote the two lengthy poems, "Venus and Adonis" and "Lucrece," and the one hundred and fifty-four sonnets and the thirty-two plays in eighteen years in which he was also actor and actor-manager and theatrical man of business, all not without success or solid enough profit in the terms of that age? He must, too, have been "gentle"; he must have had a certain capacity for sweet indifference to outer things and for tranquillity among his private friends not to have broken down long before amid the hard, violent living in the theatrical London of his day, consumed as he was by the personal passions recorded in the sonnets and no less by the rending creative and vicarious passions of the plays. The central factors of personal and creative passion have been neglected by the scholars who have written the books about Shakespeare, for the simple reason that they had experience of neither and thus little insight into the nature of one who was, almost beyond all men,

Servile to all the skyey influences.

He was born of prosperous middle-class parents in Stratford-on-Avon in 1564, and unquestionably attended the grammar school, largely and luckily then a Latin school, until the age of thirteen or fourteen when his father began to fall into financial difficulties. It is not too difficult and not conjectural in the ordinary sense—since this William Shakespeare *did* later write the sonnets and the plays—to imagine the precocious, infinitely sensitive youngster torn by all the passions lunary and sublunary with as yet no outlet either in life or work and so tempted to idleness, prankishness and such small excesses as the village offered. The first vital experience in the post-adolescent fusion of animal need and ideal striving would be that of love—love on the part of the youngster, immensely mature intellectually though emotionally so defenseless, for a girl older than himself and so perhaps apparently at least a trifle more understanding than the village girls of his own age. This trifle of supposed understanding the youth would idealize under the ardors of a clandestine passion. No wonder that at the age of eighteen he got with child the twenty-six-year-old Anne Hathaway and married her by special license—whether he liked it or not—six months before the birth of the daughter Susanna who was later to be his favorite child. He undoubtedly did not like it, however for the moment he pretended to himself, half-playing the manly part, that he did; for it is of the essence of the creative spirit to desire to be unbound and to be afraid of substituting life and biological immortality for the creative act and its projection into the future. The terror of frustration must have gripped him when promptly nine months after Susanna, twins were born, Hamnet and Judith, boy and girl. No wonder that after 1584 there is no further record of him in Stratford. He had fled. He was in London. For eight years he is lost sight of—for the eight years between twenty and twenty-eight, between youth and manhood.

The scholars have ransacked all written records of the age and racked their poor brains to verify the gossip turned to legend. Is it true that the young Shakespeare had the reputation of being a wild youth in his native village? As if it were ever *not* true of a poet, especially of one who did in the end seduce a respectable girl? Did Shakespeare have to flee for poaching in the deer park of Sir Thomas Luce, even though it is doubtful whether Luce had a deer park? It really doesn't matter. For the legend is sound in its knowledge of the fact that he had to flee and did flee, by whatever mythic circumstance it explained his flight. The contemporary gossips knew and whispered the real reason. But the legend of the poet developed according to a less sincere pattern. Better admit poaching, which was not considered a very heinous matter, than confess that a respectable man's son fled from his wife and three babies. And the respectable pillars of society are amusingly still busy and a professor of Cornell University argues that we have no proof that Shakespeare did not take his Anne and three babies to London. Of course, we have not—except the vision of Shakespeare, twenty, poor, of passion and imagination all compact, burning with all the fiercest ardors and appetites of the poetic temperament at its highest, living amid the poets and actors of that turbulent and unbridled period, grappling with that life, ultimately triumphant in both its practical and its highest creative aspects, beginning to nourish that homoerotic substitution of an ideal other self for his own and for a muse which culminates in his sonnets, as it had done in the sonnets of Michel Angelo—a vision of this Shakespeare, experiencing these things, with Anne at his lodgings, asking him in the name of his three wailing infants where he had spent the night or the day. . . .

We have not many more prosaic facts concerning him. After 1592 the records admirably and painstakingly searched by the antiquarians tell us that he had risen from whatever other and humbler employments in the theatre of his day to that of poet and playwright. In 1593 and 1594, moreover, the two longish poems, "Venus and Adonis" and "Lucrece," were published. Both were quite successful and established Shakespeare firmly among the younger poets of his period. By 1598, when he was thirty-four, Francis Meres in a sort of handbook of contemporary literature called *Palladis Tamia* speaks of Shakespeare as "the most excellent in both kinds," that is, both comedy and tragedy, calls him "the most passionate among us to bewail and bemoan the perplexities of love," and gives us the first news of his "sugared sonnets among his private friends."

From now until the retirement to Stratford in 1610 we have no outer facts to go on except the chronology of the plays as succeeding generations of scholars have established it. But this chronology does not quite tell us what the scholars would like to have it tell us, namely the story of a fairly steady development in Shakespeare's art and mind. Doubtless there is something of autumnal maturity in the character of Prospero in *The Tempest* (1611-12) but there is none at all in the charming but tricky and silly *Winter's Tale* (1610-11); there is undoubtedly a growing power in the matchless management of the blank-verse medium at the highest moments, but there is no corresponding improvement in the matter of those furiously foolish conceits which were the worst fault of all the Elizabethans and which troubled even the idolator Coleridge. Nor is the dramaturgic structure of *The Tempest* anything but a farrago of romantic accidents and coincidences. It seems right and harmonious that *Macbeth* and *Lear* should have been composed in a single season (1605-06) but the next year's play, *Antony and Cleopatra,* though bristling with divine quotations and great in its delineation of the Egyptian queen, again misses completely the comparative tightness of action and fusing of intellectual elements that mark the topmost tragedies. So, too, the "plotty" and rather trivial *Twelfth Night* belongs to the same season as *Hamlet* (1600-01) the greatest of the plays not least because the most controlledly written rather than divinely "spouted," and bracketed together for 1596-97 are *King John* and *The Merchant of Venice,* and for 1594-95 *Love's Labour's Lost* and *Romeo and Juliet,* both young and the product of youth, no doubt, but at what an interval from each other!

Does then the chronology of the scholars, which there is no reason for not substantially adopting, tell us nothing? It tells us a great deal. It tells us once more the story of the poet of dazzling natural gifts who "never blotted out a line." It confirms again that older and sounder view of Shakespeare as a man in whom genius far outshone judgment—not often a fine dramaturgic artist even within the loose form of his age, not often a writer of steady excellence or freeing himself at any but highest moments from the euphuism of his youth, no serene or tempered or self-directed spirit like Milton or Goethe, but fiery, moody, intensely uplifted or correspondingly cast down and either carelessly carpentering plays for the companies with which he was associated or else projecting upon the stage through the subject choice of the greater and profounder plays some passion that consciously or unconsciously he himself had felt. For a poet chooses one subject rather than another, or a dramatist, as in the case of Shakespeare, chooses to dramatize one tale or legend rather than another, not by chance, not by accident—there being indeed no such thing—but through some profound inner urgency, through the deep implication of the passions involved with the poet's interior life.

So what we know of Shakespeare of the years of his triumphant activity is this—at least this, though his terrifying temperament held more, of course, more that was inscrutable to him and is inscrutable forever: finding no personal muse for whom and through whom to create, for which reason his opinion of woman, for all the charm of many of those boyish virgins like Rosalind or Beatrice, is not too high, he fell into that passion for a youth which the sonnets chronicle so vividly. It matters not a jot who that youth was. He yearned, like the great Greeks, to form one to be higher than himself— to create in living human substance and not only in art. But he loved, too, and with a more embodied passion the dark lady of the sonnets and through both, the idealized youth and the dark mistress, he suffered grief and ill. He knew at least in dreams young and immortal passion that must end in death (*Romeo and Juliet*); he knew the impulse to tame even with cruelty the irrational female (*The Taming of the Shrew*); he projected his most obscure and ultimate experience of a powerful mother fixation and hatred of the father turned in compensation into an idealization of the dead father, yet wreaking itself in the killing of the father substitute, in *Hamlet;* he knew the extreme pangs of jealousy (*Othello*) and the intense urgency of ambition, though it is noteworthy that Macbeth but for the urging of the female furies on the heath and a living fury by his side would have dreamed murders rather than done them; he knew, though only forty-three, which was, however, late in his own life, the mood of failure and decay and being abandoned by both strength and love, even as Lear was, and centered the cruelty and defeat of life again in those two women, Goneril and Regan, whom he drew with so cold and exact a hatred; he knew and expressed through Prospero in *The Tempest* the self-apotheosis of creative power and the resignation of that power, partly because it is, of course, an illusion even at its highest, for tranquility and the good conventional life of ordinary mortals. We know all that concerning him. Is it not a great deal? Is it not more than if we knew what lodgings he occupied or what was the color of his hair?

From 1610 on a few records and documents begin again to speak. They speak once more of something not unfamiliar in the life of creative artists—their yearning, as already hinted at, for that from which their strangeness excludes them—settled house and stead, a place within the human and communal order, the founding of a house and tribe rather than the creation of a tribe of phantoms. "Our revels are now ended." He acquired lands in his native village and the handsomest house there and was not unlucky in this circumstance, at least, that his daughter Susanna, married to the physician John Hall, was, if the inscription on her tombstone is to be trusted, "witty above her sex" in which characteristic, as the writer of the inscription adds, there was "something of Shakespeare." His retirement to Stratford is dated 1610, so that only six years were left him for the enjoyment of that ordered life of a prominent man in his native place, of which he had dreamed, as artists often do, amid the fiery ardors and scorching pains of the creative process. He did not and could not, of course, lose touch with that truer life of his, as we know from the guests he had in his house, Michael Drayton and Ben Jonson, on that occasion when he "drank too hard" and almost at once lay down to die.

Finally we have the will revised by Shakespeare on his deathbed about which scholars, determined to save for the poet their kind of respectability, have so amusingly written. He left some fitting legacies including £10, then many times its present value, to the village poor; he left money wherewith to buy memorial rings to his best friends; he left his estate, all that he died possessed of both in Stratford and London to his daughter Susanna, but left it forever entailed upon the male heirs—"to the first son of her body lawfully issuing and to the heirs males of the body, lawfully issuing." Careless of the preservation of his works, he desired to establish a line, a clan, a house amid the landed gentry of his shire. The poet's yearning for the tranquility of the conventional life, a feeling which in our own age Thomas Mann has delineated in story after story, was in Shakespeare's heart at the end. The provision of the will which has so troubled the scholars in this: "Item, I give unto my wife my second-best bed with the furniture." They have pointed out that this meant no neglect of Anne, seeing that her dower-right in all he died possessed of was indisputable. Nor may there be much significance in the fact, discovered by the late Sidney Lee, that in 1613 Shakespeare bought a property in London on such terms as definitely to bar the widow's dower. The scholars have forgotten that Shakespeare was a poet still and not only a poet but a humorist and no profoundly self-analytic soul in the modern sense. He may himself not have known the innermost meaning of that conspicuous and sole mention of his wife in connection with what was "second-best." His subconscious knew perfectly and he himself derived a conscious satisfaction from the phrase.

[III]

At one of the heights of romantic Shakespeariolatry Matthew Arnold wrote in a sonnet, notably fine as such:

> Others abide our questions. Thou art free.
> We ask and ask: thou smilest and art still,
> Out-topping knowledge.

This has become the classical expression of the view of Shakespeare as at once all-wise and inscrutable. It has not been sufficiently observed, by the way, that these two notions are mutually exclusive. Wisdom is hardly such unless it is intelligibly communicated and he who is inscrutable keeps the secret of his wisdom to himself. But let us, remembering that poetry is both more precious and more enduring than philosophy, put a few questions on vital matters to the works of him whose life has here been interpreted as the life of poet not sage, dreamer not thinker, unselfconscious genius in an unintellectual and fiery age.

From this questioning the comedies, except *The Merchant of Venice* (1594), *Measure for Measure* (1604) and *The Tempest* (1611), must be omitted. In these three instances a graver theme evoked a graver and more responsible mood. Especially in the first of these three there is found a sobriety in the method of characterization almost unmatched except in *Hamlet, Macbeth* and *Othello*. The other eleven comedies from *Love's Labour's Lost* (1591) to *The Winter's Tale* (1611) withdraw themselves from such questioning by what they are. For they invite comparison neither with reality nor with any coherent structure of the imagination. Their world has no logic even of its own nor is it transposed into a purposeful stylization. It is an imaginatively irresponsible world, a tricksy and haphazard one. It glitters with wit; it glows at moments with lyricism both rich and poignant. But of these wildly arbitrary resemblances, coincidences, undiscovered practices of transvestism, unmotivated conversions, the last word must be that of Fabian in *Twelfth Night:* "If this were played upon a stage now, I would condemn it as improbable fiction." There is indeed—and this is the point—no attempt at probability, no effort to convince either the reason or the imagination or the heart.

The writing answers the matter. Immortal beauty flashes from these gleeful, exuberant and abandoned pages:

> Many can brook the weather that love not the wind,

or

> A woman moved is like a fountain troubled,

or

> He dies to me again when talked of . . .

or

    Cleanse the foul body of the infected world.

But these flashes—and there are a thousand—are indeed flashes. They are sudden golden threads in a texture without firm anterior design. The wit, too, flashes suddenly. At times it is keen and deep: "I'll be drunk with those that have the fear of God, and not with drunken knaves." At times it is imaginative, as in Falstaff's remark: "I should have been a mountain of mummy." But vast stretches of it are the same kind of clowning: "Welcome the sour cup of prosperity! Affliction may one day smile again." It answers two descriptions which Shakespeare himself furnished. "A fine volley of words," says Sylvia in the *Two Gentlemen of Verona*, "and quickly shot off." Beside which may be set Viola's line from *Twelfth Night*: "They that dally nicely with words may quickly make them wanton."

The Shakespeare of the comedies is like a virtuoso of matchless brilliance, enchanted with his instrument, dazzled by his medium. It is all fresh and new to him, including his own virtuosity. He improvises; he is charmed out of himself by the mere succession of sounds; old phrases or variations on them occur, but since there is no control from within, it matters nothing and the player finds his compensation in the unrivaled wealth of musical combinations that he commands and that show no sign of a diminishing abundance until the day comes on which he lays aside the lyre forever. In

the *Two Gentlemen of Verona* (1591) Launce says:
"She hath more qualities than a water-spaniel—which is
much in a bare Christian." In *The Winter's Tale* (1611)
the Clown, supposedly in Bohemia, speaks of the song-
men at the shearers' festival: "They are most of them
means and bases; but one puritan amongst them, and he
sings psalms to horn-pipes."

We may now question the plays that will bear to be
questioned. There are, needless to say, flashes of sudden
insight. All fundamental problems flickered on the horizon of the poet's mind. Thus the problem of value and
the foundations of value. The question is debated between Hector and Troilus in *Troilus and Cressida*
whether Helen, the cause of the Trojan war, should not
simply be returned to the Greeks.

> *Hect.* Brother, she is not worth what she doth cost
>   The holding.
> *Tro.*   What is aught but as 'tis valued?
>   But value dwells not in particular will;
>   It holds his estimate and dignity
>   As well wherein 'tis precious in itself
>   As in the prizer.

A brave beginning of a great argument. But it issues
in neither continuing thought nor resultant action. The
flash darkens as swiftly as it came. We are dealing with
a poet and a hurried man of the theatre, too, who had
largely to take opinion, *Weltanschaung,* if any one likes,
ready-made from the intellectual climate of his age and

give it forth in what was far more powerful in him than any will toward meaning, namely the will toward speech and form.

What is man's ultimate fate? The lines in *Hamlet* are universally known. Who would endure this "weary life"

> But that the dread of something after death,
> The undiscovered country from whose bourn
> No traveller returns, puzzles the will,
> And makes us rather bear those ills we have
> Than fly to others that we know not of?

Well, but did not his father's ghost tell Hamlet he is

> confined to fast in fires,
> Till the foul crimes done in my days of nature
> Are burnt and purged away,

in other words, that he is in Purgatory and that he is so partly, at least, because he died

> Unhousel'd, disappointed, unaneled,

that is to say, without host or holy anointing or the final Catholic rites of the dying. Then why Hamlet's question, if he believes the ghost? And were the Danes of that age Catholic? Shakespeare probably asked himself none of these questions. He worked as a poet of the theatre within the acceptable traditions of his time. What did he himself believe? In all likelihood he did not know. Claudio in *Measure for Measure* engages in the same speculation on the same terms:

> Ay, but to die, and go we know not where;
> To lie in cold obstruction and to rot.

That is a universal terror. But Claudio goes on:

> To bathe in fiery floods, or to reside
> In thrilling regions of thick-ribbed ice;
> To be imprisoned in the viewless winds,
> And blown with restless violence round about
> The pendent world; or to be worse than worst
> Of those that lawless and incertain thought
> Imagine howling.

It is a Dantesque medieval hell that is here delineated. But note the element of doubt. It is "lawless and incertain thought" that imagines the dead howling in hell. It may be objected that these utterances are dramatic. But Hamlet is closest interwoven of all the characters and plays for demonstrable psychological reasons with the poet himself, and Claudio is no well-defined character at all but any young man torn between opposing terrors. Moreover, all that is written in any book, however transformed into its manifest meaning by the conscious art of the writer, has its latent meaning inseparable from the substance of the writer's soul. Shakespeare neither believed nor disbelieved. His moods dictated his fears and hopes. Closest to the pagan groundwork of his soul were probably those final lines of Claudio which are an extraordinary echo of the words which in the underworld of shades Achilles addressed to Odysseus:

> The weariest and most loathed worldly life
> That age, ache, penury and imprisonment
> Can lay on nature is a paradise
> To what we fear of death.

For every human mood and every human fear and every human passion Shakespeare has the highest, most energetic, most memorable expression. His highest virtue is properly understood almost a lyrical virtue. Of fixed wisdom or guided thought neither the poet nor the works had any.

Let us address one other question to his works. And it will be amusing to make that the question concerning the structure and justice of the social order. For if they have not already done so, the so-called Marxist critics will doubtless claim Shakespeare for their own. The historical plays will be difficult to explain or explain away. For they trouble even one who is far enough removed from Marxist theory or proletarian thought. These kings and queens and dukes and earls in this great pageant full of pomp and panoply and both war's glitter and alarm are of a rigid and intolerable arrogance. They are, in their own persons, denominated England, France, Burgundy, Austria. The lands are their private domains; the peoples are their chattels, good enough to be loyal to their lieges and die for them in these portentous and yet meaningless private quarrels of passion, ambition or mere untutored rage. And the thing that is true of the historical plays is true no less of the great tragedies. We hear nothing of the people of

Scotland in *Macbeth* nor of the Britains in *Lear* nor of the consequences to them of change of rulers or the arbitrary division of realms. The social morality of all these plays is pre-prophetic, almost pre-Noachic. No Nathan or Jeremiah ever shakes the conscience of these rulers. Remote, ceremonious and bloody, they undergo that human fate of mutability of which Shakespeare and the men of his age never thought in connection with the lot of humbler men:

> Sceptre and crown must tumble down
> And in the dust be equal made
> By the poor crooked scythe and spade.

Once only, except for moments in the Roman plays, and then for a few brief scenes, the populace breaks in. There had been the not quite ineffectual uprising of the Kentishmen under Jack Cade in 1450, and Shakespeare duly chronicles it in the second part of *King Henry VI*. He chronicles it superbly. He chronicles it with that touch of exquisite and superior malice which, as has not been sufficiently observed, marks all his dealings with the lower classes. He knows, to speak in modern parlance, the psychology of the mob. Listen to Cade winning the populace to his side:

There shall be in England seven halfpenny loaves sold for one penny; the three-hooped pot shall have ten hoops; and I will make it felony to drink small beer. . . . There shall be no money; all shall eat and drink; and I will apparel them all in one livery, that they may agree like brothers and worship me their lord.

He announces, needless to say, that "henceforward all things shall be in common." One of his followers cries: "The first thing to do, let's kill all the lawyers." All things shall be in common except one thing—culture. Even Shakespeare's proletarians objected to what since has been called bourgeois ideology. "He can speak French and therefore he is a traitor!" And again: "It will be proved to thy face that thou hast men about thee that usually talk of a noun and a verb, and such abominable words as no Christian ear can endure to hear." At last even Cade is impatient with his followers: "Was ever feather so lightly blown to and fro as this multitude?" Is there any doubt that Shakespeare agreed upon the whole with the authorities of the kingdom that Cade and his rabble were

> Rebellious hinds, the filth and scum of Kent
> Mark'd for the gallows?

But it cannot have escaped any attentive readers that Shakespeare's comic characters, with a few exceptions such as the half-mystic figure of the Fool in *Lear,* are drawn from the class of "clowns" and "hinds" and "servingmen and women" and that, legitimately enough, no small part of the comic effect is due to the ignorance of the people, an ignorance largely verbal, too, and to the simplicity of their inner processes? That is true of Launcelot Gobbo in *The Merchant of Venice;* it is true of the justly immortal Dogberry and Verges in *Much Ado About Nothing* and of that whole scene of theirs which begins with Dogberry's question: "Is our whole dissembly appeared?" and ends with his cry: "O that I had been writ down an ass!" It is no less true of the almost equally amusing Elbow in *Measure for Measure*, another constable, with his marrowy: "O thou caitiff! O thou varlet! O thou wicked Hannibal! I was respected to her before I was married to her! If ever I was respected with her, or she with me, let not your worship think me the poor Duke's officer. Prove this, thou wicked Hannibal, or I'll have mine action of battery on thee!" Shakespeare's delineation of the inner life of the lower classes is subtler than that of their clowning and their malapropisms. But even then he laughs at and not with them, though in no unkindly spirit. Coleridge has finely remarked that the Nurse in *Romeo and Juliet* remembers things by the concatenation of trivial incidents and not, as educated people do, by the association of ideas. This discovery made by Shakespeare and later used or rediscovered by Molière and by Dickens is most magnificently and unforgettably exemplified not by the Nurse in *Romeo and Juliet* but by Mistress Quickly in the second part of *King Henry IV*, when she marvelously answers the question of Sir John Falstaff: "What is the gross sum that I owe thee?"

"Marry, if thou wert an honest man, thyself and the money too. Thou didst swear to me upon a parcel-gilt goblet, sitting in my Dolphin-chamber, at the round table, by a sea-coal fire, upon Wednesday in Whitsun week, when the prince broke thy head for liking his father to a singing man of

Windsor, thou didst swear to me then, as I was washing thy wound, to marry me and make me my lady thy wife. Canst thou deny it? Did not goodwife Keech, the butcher's wife, come in then and call me gossip Quickly? coming in to borrow a mess of vinegar; telling us she had a good dish of prawns; whereby thou didst desire to eat some; whereby I told thee they were ill for a green wound? And didst thou not desire me when she was gone downstairs, to be no more so familiar with such poor people; saying that ere long they should call me madam? And did thou not kiss me and bid me fetch thee thirty shillings? I put thee now to thy book-oath; deny it, if thou canst."

He had no metaphysical opinions of his own—this fiery, romantic, impassioned poet who watched human comedy and tragedy as a pageant that passed before his eyes; he had no especial political or social views, but accepted both the world and the world order, as they were, having no high opinion of either, but seeing no good in change nor really dreaming of it, not above drawing from that order the good it might bring him, even as his will shows, in the form of a name, an estate, and men to bear that name and hold those lands amid their fellows in the times to come. He probably shared the critical views of his time to the effect that poetry and so, too, the poetical drama were but a handsome kind of feign- ing, worthy of grave men only in so far as a moral lesson could be derived therefrom. Nor did he in the slightest rebel against this last notion. Everywhere in the plays vice comes to grief; nemesis overtakes the excesses and errors of the virtuous, as it overtakes Lear and Othello; rarely as in Cordelia's death is there blank and inexplicable tragedy. Nor does he inquire into the laws under which human justice is meted out but accepts them as they are. He might conceivably be said to have been very English under these aspects, more so than the proud and rebellious Milton. He played the game. His works were pageant, were vision, were dream and, with that pessimism ever at the core of even the noblest pagan hearts, he could finally declare that:

> like the baseless fabric of this vision,
> The cloud-capp'd towers, the gorgeous palaces,
> The solemn temples, the great globe itself,
> Yea, all which it inherit, shall dissolve,
> And, like this insubstantial pageant faded,
> Leave not a rack behind. We are such stuff
> As dreams are made on; and our little life
> Is rounded with a sleep.

[IV]

He was the supreme poet of the expression of the passions of man. He was neither sage nor politician. Nor was he in the sense of either Sophocles or Ibsen a dramatic artist with a sense of form and of the significance of that form. But why should he have been, except for the urge of the modern pedagogue to have something above criticism to teach? He did appear, as Johnson rightly said "when Learning's triumph o'er her

barbarous foes *first* rear'd the stage." He had no tradition of a severe dramatic art to lean on and the very
great creators are never innovators but take for their
expression existing forms. So he adopted the loose,
plotty technique of his time, full of unnecessary mis-
understandings, of disguises, of what is now called the
"frame-up," of lost objects and mistaken identities and
ended his actions in most cases when it was time for the
spectators to go home with sudden conversions or discoveries; or brought about tragic catastrophe, as in
Romeo and Juliet, by the device of a letter which acci-
dentally did not reach in time. Voltaire was not wrong
in those strictures of his. The trouble was that he did
not see Shakespeare in the setting of his age but merely
by the side of the neoclassic tragedy of the French. The
truth is that perhaps only and alone in *Lear* and *Macbeth* and *Julius Caesar* and *Hamlet* does the dramatic
pattern—and then only when stripped of its excres-
cences and superfluities—coincide, as it does in Sophocles
and Ibsen, with the inherent moral or intellectual pattern of character from which the action springs.

These things, moreover, cohere; they are one. A tight
form is the outward projection of an inner congruity of
thought and view; a vehement passion may flame and
smolder alternately or, growing weary, burn for a space
with an idle and desultory fire. A spearlike thought or
vision of the moral world will fling itself straight at its
appointed target. So it is not strange that Shakespeare's
general form is as loose and arbitrary as the plots into

which he weaves his fables. This is not often perceived because he persuades us by the sheer magic of the word. Masses of euphuistic verbiage there are, but suddenly out of their midst there issues a passage so soaring and so memorable that the context of both structure and style fade from the memory and only the glory of that high poetic eloquence remains. But a cool examination of one or two average Shakespearean plots and structures will show us why he could not have been a great dramaturgic artist, by which, of course, is meant not an able purveyor of stage material for the theatre of his moment in history but one whose dramatic idea builds itself a spire of form from within.

Take *Measure for Measure*. The Duke—here called, for no reason, of Vienna—chooses to relinquish his power for a while and disappear. He makes Angelo his deputy

> Lent him our terror, dress'd him with our love.

Angelo revives old statutes, "blue laws," one of which provides the death penalty for extramarital intercourse. A young man named Claudio, having gotten with child his sweetheart Julietta whom, however, he had every intention of marrying and had not yet legally married merely because of property interests involved, is arrested on a capital charge. Claudio sends his sister Isabella, who is about to take conventual vows, to intercede with Angelo. He, though betrothed to Marianna who dwells at the moated grange, conceives so violent a passion for

Isabella that he offers her the choice between her chastity and her brother's life. From this situation of tense danger and choice there issue the two famous and central scenes between Isabella and Angelo and between Isabella and Claudio. In both scenes the dramatic emphasis is on the sacredness of chastity and on whether or not Isabella should prefer her honor to her brother's life. In neither scene does anyone attack the ultimate cause of the conflict—the arbitrariness of power and of whimsically delegated power to affect and ruin human lives. Isabella in a famous passage inveighs against Angelo's wicked *use* of his power:

> Man, proud man,
> Drest in a little brief authority,
> Most ignorant of what he's most assured,
> His glassy essence, like an angry ape,
> Plays such fantastic tricks before high heaven
> As make the angels weep.

She never questions Angelo's right to that little brief authority, nor the Duke's right to delegate it to him, nor the right of the governors to decree cruel and unjust laws and let them lapse and arbitrarily revive them. Nor does Claudio. Shakespeare, in brief, accepts the world at its most conventional. He never grapples with the idea behind the action, with the principles of life from which tragic entanglements *ought* or ought *not* to arise. He plays the game and stays within it. Here we know, to be sure, that near as we skirt tragedy we shall only skirt it. But the device is childlike and as in a fairy tale. The Duke, disguised as a friar, wanders in and out of the play and finally, all fundamentals being left where they were, not only forgives Angelo but marries Isabella. It would be to "break a butterfly upon a wheel" to ask why the nunlike Isabella is willing to marry the Duke.

How Shakespeare could repress in his own soul and cause to be repressed by good men through the ages elementary moral values by the dazzling glory of his word and the enchantment of his passion is best illustrated by *The Merchant of Venice*. There is no quarrel with his sharing the conception of his age regarding the wicked Jewish usurer, next door to the devil himself, especially since his supreme though unconscious instinctive humanity made him place a plea on Shylock's lips and give Shylock other words and moods which temper, if indeed they do not break from within, the traditional demonic figure. In the delineation of Shylock he rose beyond his age. But what of Bassanio, a self-confessed idler and spendthrift who, having first squandered his own patrimony and next thrown away his heavy borrowings from Antonio, his devoted friend, now asks for further loans in order to gamble on the possibility of a rich marriage with an heiress he has not seen? He consents, after some polite hesitation, to the loan from Shylock upon these dangerous terms, though to him and Antonio, Shylock is necessarily evil and necessarily—they would not even have it otherwise—an implacable enemy. And all Venice knows of this bargain and all Venice knows of Antonio's misfortunes and no one, no one of all this company, comes forward to advance the three thousand ducats before the extreme moment had come. Such were the lovers and the friends of that once "royal merchant." That one of them eloped not only with the adversary's daughter but with the adversary's pearls and that Antonio himself consents in the end not only to use one-half of the fruits of Shylock's wicked usury but insists that Shylock "presently become a Christian," that is, be driven to profess something he cannot and will not believe—these details but confirm, granting Shakespeare and his age *their* Shylock, the puerile and deplorable ethical mood. Yet this very discussion at the end of three centuries and a half is a supreme tribute not to Shakespeare the thinker or the thinking dramaturgist—he was neither—but to the imperishable beauty and vitality of that verbal and human texture, above all to that magic word, by which he has lulled the generations into sharing his rich and eloquent dreams.

It would be no malicious criticism that examined all of Shakespeare's plots and ethical methods and assumptions after this fashion. For the purpose of such a proceeding would be to illustrate his triumph despite puerile devices—the handkerchief in *Othello,* the undelivered letter in *Romeo and Juliet,* the sudden conversion of Duke Frederick at the end of *As You Like It* —despite untenable ethical assumptions, despite the central fact that, being intellectually wholly of his age, he never rose from the conception of a conflict *within* accepted notions to a conflict in which the validity of those notions was itself the dramatic crux and core. . . . Except in *Hamlet*. Except in that one intimate and incommensurable work which came from the ultimate depth of personality. All through the works there are evidences of Shakespeare's uncommonly strong father complex. Its traces are in *Lear*, stronger traces are in the relation of Brutus to Caesar in *Julius Caesar*, a remarkably tight play, intensely wrought, and preceding *Hamlet* by but a season. Hatred of the father transformed into a defensive idealization, jealousy of the father's rights, passionate attachment to the mother —these are in varying degrees common factors in human character and destiny. Hamlet meets another and also not uncommon, though somewhat rarer fate, which never fails to wring the soul to its depths. His father dies; at last the psychical possession of the mother seems in sight. But she remarries and the son's universe crumbles—as it did for Baudelaire to whom this thing happened, as it does for the finely imagined figure of Spandrell in Aldous Huxley's *Point Counter Point*. Note with what excesses of self-torture Hamlet dwells again and again on the brutal physical aspect of his mother's second marriage. He cannot endure it; these images goad him; they stand between him and Ophelia. He becomes consciously recessive. It is not so much the time that is out of joint as his personal world. He cannot face it; he cannot endure it. For there is another difficulty. The murderer of his father and hated bedfellow of his mother is his father's brother and so symbolizes the father to him and some of the feeling of guilt that turned hatred of the father into an exorbitant admiration and love fixes itself upon Claudius. Thence springs the deepest motive for Hamlet's hesitation. The queen understands dimly but with certainty:

> I doubt it is no other but the main;
> His father's death and our o'erhasty marriage.

Hamlet too knows that his hesitation has a deeper and obscurer source than any of his rationalizations. He doubts the very ghost whom he has seen and whom the powers of evil may have wrought

> Out of my weakness and my melancholy.

And he must die. He cannot kill the king until his own death is certain, because he could not bear the harrowing guilt of killing the symbol of his father toward whom so much anterior guilt had already been assumed. So in this play the very accidents and shallow stage devices—the rage of Laertes, the poisoned foils—are instruments of a profound spiritual and *therefore* dramaturgic necessity. Here ultimate depths had been opened; a deeper revelation flashes on Hamlet just before his end:

> Had I but time—ah, this fell sergeant, death,
> Is strict in his arrest—O, I could tell you—
> But let it be.

The rest had to be silence. No longer were these things uttered as in the days of Oedipus and his poet.

All subject choices on the part of the poet are dictated by inner necessity. But that necessity may come from different psychical strata. Shakespeare's choice of this subject came from the deepest stratum of his psyche. It is his play. Hamlet is close to Shakespeare; the "sweet prince" of Horatio's farewell is like the "gentle" poet whom Ben Jonson knew. He is the most intimately represented of all the characters; he is—has it not been noted?—the only cultured philosophic gentleman in all the plays, a poet and a scholar, an expert on Shakespeare's own sister arts of acting and the theatre, subtle, the contemporary of the spirits of all ages, courteous and kind, critical of the ways of the society into which he was born—a creature of a different species from those noble barbarians Othello or Lear or Macbeth and equally different from those poetic but brainless romantics, like Romeo, who furnish so large a part of the population of the world of the plays. His uniqueness in the Shakespearean world has never been sufficiently emphasized. He alone shrinks from love, as philosophically Shakespeare did:

> The expense of spirit in a waste of shame
> Is lust in action.

He cannot separate himself from the mother image, even as the young Shakespeare sought the mother image in an older woman. He clings to Horatio, as

Shakespeare did for so long to the friend of the sonnets.
He is full of inexplicable inner difficulties, as is none
other in that vast company of men and women, and as
every creative spirit is and as Shakespeare was. And so
it is no wonder that to the sensitive ear there is, outside
of certain sonnets, no passage in all the works that floats
across the centuries with an accent so personal, so re-
vealing and so freighted with the pathos of a living
voice as Hamlet's final adjuration to his friend of
friends:

> If thou didst ever hold me in thy heart,
> Absent thee from felicity a while,
> And in this harsh world draw thy breath in pain,
> To tell my story.

[V]

The gentle, fiery translunary poet who revealed himself most deeply in the play *Hamlet* and in the sonnets,
but who was neither a sage nor a great or even good
dramaturgic artist, triumphs over time primarily
through his gift of embodying passion in eternal speech.
He has no continuous excellence of texture. Once more
it is *Hamlet* which almost alone is free from cold ex-
travagance, clotted conceits, needless masses of intricate
verbiage. But from this unequal stylistic texture there
arise a thousand times words that fix ultimate human
passion once and forever and so transfix the heart of
mankind. And first and highest and most characteristic

are those great laconic expressions of the Vergilian *lacrimae rerum,* the tears of mortal things, the pathos of man's fate. Such are Macduff's words on his murdered wife and children:

> I cannot but remember such things were,
> That were most precious to me;

such is the cry of Lear:

> You see me here, you gods, a poor old man,
> As full of grief as rage;

such is the speech of Edgar in *Lear* at sight of his blinded father:

> I would not take this from report: it is,
> And my heart breaks at it.

Such, in the last scene of *Othello,* are those incomparable lines placed in the mouth of Emilia, one of the few women in Shakespeare who has a heart and a mind:

> Thou hast not half that power to do me harm
> As I have to be hurt;

and the marvelously tense and ominous line:

> Perchance, Iago, I will ne'er go home;

and such is the Moor's unforgettable cry:

> O ill-starr'd wench!
> Pale as thy smock!

From the unequally written and ill-constructed play of *Antony and Cleopatra* they rise—these immortal flashes:

I am so lated in the world that I
Have lost my way forever,

Antony laments. They corruscate in the sky over the dying Cleopatra:

O sun,
Burn the great sphere thou movest in! darkling stand
The varying shore of the world:

and better still:

And there is nothing left remarkable
Beneath the visiting moon;

and best of all:

No more, but e'en a woman, and commanded
By such poor passion as the maid that milks
And does the meanest chares.

He drives deep into the human heart and sums up what all have felt and all may feel in such fashion that thereafter only silence seems fit. He turns with undiminished power at his high moments from verse to prose and Hamlet's apostrophe to man and Shylock's defense of himself and his people, both in prose, are—medium for medium—not below the most exalted passages in verse. Nor does he in this highest expression of human passion limit himself as in the brief laconic passages above to love and loss and death. He is the master in speech of the whole range of human emotion from the celebration of his native land by John of Gaunt in *Richard II* to the moonlit verbal serenades in the epi-

logue act of *The Merchant of Venice;* from the terrifying doubts that shake Banquo's soul:

> Fears and scruples shake us:
> In the great hand of God I stand—

and the equally terrifying remorse and despair of Macbeth to the question that Hamlet asks of eternity itself;
and from the bitter, grief-stricken subtleties of Antony
over the body of Caesar and the angry stabs and thrusts
of the quarrel between Brutus and Cassius to the didactic generalizing seven ages of man as described by
Jacques in *As You Like It.* These are a few and but a
few of the topmost heights and there are many that fall
not too far below. Yet it is almost needless to say that
the memory of men clings most closely to the magic
word of Shakespeare where it deals with the central
and universal and kindred mysteries of love and death
—Eros and Thanatos—as they blend in those last words
of Othello:

> When you shall these unlucky deeds relate,
> Speak of me as I am; nothing extenuate,
> Nor set down aught in malice; then, must you speak
> Of one that loved not wisely but too well;
> Of one not easily jealous, but, being wrought,
> Perplex'd in the extreme; of one whose hand,
> Like the base Indian, threw a pearl away
> Richer than all his tribe; of one whose subdued eyes
> Albeit unused to the melting mood,
> Drop tears as fast as the Arabian trees

Their medicinal gum. Set you down this;
And say besides, that in Aleppo once,
Where a malignant and a turban'd Turk
Beat a Venetian and traduc'd the state,
I took by the throat the circumcised dog
And smote him, thus!

The very accents and breathings of the tragic voice of the tormented pagan creature, of man, the eternal, natural, pitiful, divided, self-divided, self-tormenting, hot, bloody, ultimately and vainly repentant—these are in that passage of which each phrase, coinciding with the breathings of that halting voice, holds and commemorates forevermore an aspect of the perplexities of mortal passion, confusion, pity, shame. Such is the enchantment—literally: enchantment—of the magic word at its highest. And of that highest enchantment Shakespeare remains the unrivaled master.

GOETHE AND OUR TIME

[I]

In the spring of 1932 when, somewhat feebly and desul-
torily, the one hundredth anniversary of Goethe's death
was commemorated, it was the late Paul Valéry who at
the Sorbonne and in the presence of the President of
the Third Republic pronounced the formal discourse in
honor of the poet's memory. The choice of M. Valéry,
as well as his acceptance of the task, must have been
officially motivated. For Valéry admitted at the outset
that Goethe wrote in a language which he "was un-
happily ignorant of," so that the poet's stir and harmony
came to him only "across the veil of translations."

In view of this shattering disadvantage, seeing that
the French translations of Goethe are even worse than
those in English, Valéry acquitted himself admirably
well. Neither the exquisite penetration of his mind nor
the flashing swordplay of his style wholly deserted him.
He made some keen and fresh, although overemphatic
observations. Upon the whole, he had to confine himself
to the Goethe legend, as it had been created by generations of scholars and by the common herd of German
snobs who wanted to aggrandize the national poet in
terms of their sordid notions. Thus M. Valéry said: "One
says: Goethe, as one says: Orpheus—and instantly his

name imposes upon and engenders in the mind a prodigious figure—a monster of comprehension and of creative force—a monster of vitality, a monster of mobility, a monster of serenity." A little later in his discourse Valéry continues the characterization in the same vein, speaking of "this hero, this very handsome man (*ce très bel homme*), this creature terribly alive, this rather unbridled voluptuary (*ce voluptueux assez éffréné*). . . ." Then comes the climax concerning Goethe's later years: "He felt himself becoming a supreme and lucid Jupiter of ivory and gold—*un suprême et lucide Jupiter d'ivoire et d'or.*" How musically the French phrases glide! How little surprising it was that a brash, rising, ignorant young American critic of those days wrote in the *Nation* that Goethe must have been "a stuffed shirt." It was a piece of inordinate cheek and frivolity. In view of most of the things that were being said and the quality of the translations that were being produced, the brash young man's irritation was understandable.

Now Goethe was aware—as how could he not have been?—of the fact that Nature or God's grace—he would have accepted either word and concept—had given him incomparable gifts. He could not but regard with dismay the dissolution of such an organism such as his, and frankly said so. He pleased himself occasionally in his later years with the role of the half-mystic sage, the Merlin, he of whom it could be said:

> Till old experience do attain
> To something like prophetic strain.

He also, though somewhat out of shyness and the desire
not to be involved, played the role of a great gentleman.
And the key to this aspect of his character was his remark to the painter Moritz Oppenheim, that a decora-
tion and a title stand between a man and many a rough
jolt in such a world as the present. But the deeper significance is the fact that when he assumed these guises
they were not only guises. They answered to an inner
reality. He was a great sage, so great a sage that his
wisdom transcends the era in which he was born and
the era into which he survived and comes, as we shall
see, to meet the sore and bitter needs of our own time.
And he was, not in the artificial but in the truest sense,
a great gentleman—great enough to sit in shirt sleeves
among his private friends and drink more wine than
was good for him and send great ladies packing; great
enough to fulfill scrupulously every duty that life
seemed to lay on him, to the point of weariness, of
despair; great enough, under the very modest pomp of
that house on the *Frauenplan,* never to have neglected
the maxim of all maxims found in the Astrologer's lines
in the First Act of the Second Part of *Faust:*

> Wer Gutes will, der sei erst gut.
> (He who would will the good, let him first be good.)

Finally we are not without his own quite sober summing up of the whole matter. And since the Conversa-
tions with Eckermann are in all hands, this summing up
of January 27, 1824, might have given pause to all those

who spun on the Apollonian and the Jovian legends. "I
have been called a great favorite of fortune, and I am
unwilling to complain and to criticize the course my
life has taken, but at the bottom I have had nothing
but toil and trouble and I can truly say that in my
seventy-five years I have not had four weeks of entire
ease . . . I have found my true happiness in creative
meditation and accomplishment. And yet how that was
always interrupted, limited, hindered by my position
in the world . . . A wide renown and a high position
in life are good things, yet even these have advanced
me no farther than that I must be silent when others
speak their mind, in order not to wound them."

How did the legend of the "supreme and lucid Jupiter
of gold and ivory" arise? Innocently enough at first. On
March 22, 1831, precisely one year before the day of
Goethe's death, there came to pay his respects to the
great poet and Privy Councillor and Minister of the
Duke, a young man named Dr. Johann Gustav Stickel.
He must have been a very bright young man for,
though only twenty-six, he had just been appointed to
a professorship (*extraordinarius* or associate) of the-
ology and Oriental languages at the University of Jena.
He was received in Goethe's small and extremely aus-
tere study. The aged poet had a very sore foot and sat
sideways on one chair, resting the aching limb on a
second. Stickel explained to Goethe, who had been an
ardent student of the Old Testament all his life, his own
method of linguistic exegesis. So the conversation

· 112 ·

turned naturally to Oriental poetry, and this subject in turn led to Goethe's *West-Eastern Divan*. Now what our young Dr. Stickel did not know was that the cold reception accorded to the *West-Eastern Divan* had never ceased to trouble and to disappoint Goethe throughout the fifteen years since its publication. Precisely like Milton, though with a self-assurance far less categorical, Goethe knew the quality of his work. He knew that the two hundred and forty-eight lyrics and epigrams which make up the *West-Eastern Divan* form in all likelihood the greatest book of verse in its kind in all literature. He knew that these pieces lacked the freshness as of dew or dawn of his earlier lyrics; he knew no less well that for the divine limpidness and lucidity of those poems he had been able to compensate by unrivaled depth, subtlety, irony, visionary penetration, and had been able to incarnate these in forms *aere perennius,* more lasting than brass. And the book had fallen flat. And foolish reviewers had produced, as they do still, their customary mixture of pompous ignorance and malice. How was young Professor Stickel to know all that? With a kind of wide-eyed fidelity he reports what Goethe said to him, namely, that in respect of the *West-Eastern Divan* dissensions or discords (*Mishelligkeiten*) had arisen, which had induced Goethe to determine to "emigrate to some far land."

"To emigrate to some far land!" Of course, Goethe never meant it. Equally, of course, the young professor did not know that this phrase was to Goethe the ex-

pression of ultimate weariness, disgust, disillusion; that
he had used it twice before: once during the Napole-
onic Wars and once when he had come back to Weimar
from Marienbad in September 1823 and had been forced
to resign his last dream

Of youth and bloom and this delightful world.

And so, innocently, young Stickel relates how he com-
plimented Goethe on the admirable translation of an
Arabic poem printed in the "notes and dissertations"
accompanying the *West-Eastern Divan*. Whereupon
Goethe "raised his head. Although seated, it seemed as
though his form increased more and more in stature.
Loftily and majestically, like an Olympian Zeus, he began to recite."

What caused Goethe's gesture and the force of his
declamation was clearly the young admirer's healing
touch upon the scar of an old wound. Within the situation there was far more of the *lacrimae rerum* than of
Olympian majesty and indifference. And indeed the
aged poet had little enough reason for Olympian calm,
or to be that "monster of serenity" which Paul Valéry
found in the silly legend. Five months before the date
of the Stickel interview there had reached Goethe the
news of the death of his only son in Rome. August von
Goethe had always been an unhappy creature, a neurotic, a misfit. His father loved him with a more troubled
love on that account. Eight months of "dread and
doubt," as Goethe wrote of the son to old friends, had

preceded the blow which he tried, as was his wont, to accept with dignity and with no outward show of grief. And so, as had also happened to him before, the body spoke for the repressed soul and a violent hemorrhage drove him, as he wrote to Schopenhauer's sister "ankle-deep into the Lethean stream." Once more, though in his eighty-second year, he defeated death and once more shouldered all the burdens, domestic and business, which he had gradually placed in August's hands. Nine days after the Stickel interview, he noted in his diaries: "Went through the monthly bills and tabulated them," even as, barely recovered from that desperate illness he had noted on December 27 of the previous year: "I gave the coachman the key to the woodshed and had him bring wood into the house for all fireplaces. Then got the key back." In the evenings Ottilie, his daughter-in-law, who returned his long affection, read Plutarch to him. He encouraged the grandchildren to confide in him and to play in his study. Meanwhile he labored at the completion of *Faust* and at other tasks. Occasionally he needed solitude. So, sixteen days after the Stickel interview, there is the following entry in the diary: "Drove down to the Garden house. Ate by myself and reflected on all necessary affairs." The picture is that of a great man, of a man of power and goodness, of one touched, perhaps, more than most mortals, by tragedy and care. The image of the "Jupiter of ivory and gold" is evidently the reflection in a distorting mirror.

No, Goethe was not the "monster of serenity" which M. Valéry borrowed from the legend. He hid his agitations from human view and then paid heavily enough for that rigid self-discipline. Neither was he, above all, the "rather unbridled voluptuary" of Valéry's description. Handsome he was or rather, as we know from an hundred witnesses, of an irresistible charm and vivacity in his youth; age brought him, as early as after the return from Italy, a certain rigidity and stiffness of demeanor which melted into majesty as the long years went on. The notion that he was a Don Juan type, like Byron, a notion which has so troubled the English-speaking world from Wordsworth on, arose, one must conjecture, from his misinterpreted confessions, from rumor and from the single circumstance that he did not marry Christiane Vulpius, the mother of his son, until that son was old enough to be a witness of the marriage ceremony. Beyond that, the facts are far subtler and sadder than the legend implies.

It has been said that Goethe never possessed any of the women he loved most—neither Friedrike Brion nor Lily Schoenemann nor Frau von Stein nor Minna Herzlieb nor Mariane von Willemer nor Ulrike von Levetzow. If there is a shadow of doubt concerning this statement, it can be only—though we have no proof—in the case of Charlotte von Stein. In all the other cases it is certain. Whenever an attachment threatened to involve a final seriousness, Goethe fled. And he fled, consciously motivated, no doubt, by an extreme reluctance to surrender his human and creative freedom. But in that darkness which is in every human soul, a darkness of which he was by no means ignorant, there dwelt that powerful fixation on his sister Cornelia. With her he identified woman after woman, openly and clearly Charlotte von Stein, and was deterred from any consummation by the incest fear. The only reason one is inclined to question the all-inclusive statement in respect of Charlotte is because it seems unimaginable as well as melancholy that during the best years of any human life, the years from twenty-five to thirty-eight, this most vital and gifted of men lived in a state of merely psychical thralldom to a woman seven years his senior, highly intelligent, to be sure, keen in her insight into his nature, but married, ailing and of uncertain temper.

Finally, of course, this relationship nearly broke him. It was from it that he fled to Italy; it was in relief and release from it that he felt newborn and whole under those milder skies. One is glad to learn that in the second winter of his Roman sojourn he found a certain Faustina, whoever she may have been, so that he was able to write to his friend and patron, the Duke Karl August, in a letter long extant but carefully neglected by scholars and biographers, that "moderate exercise of this kind refreshes the soul," and to be able to add: "I have experienced this fact several times in my life. I have also, on the contrary, felt the discomfort of leaving the broad path and entering upon the narrow one of continency and safety." These are scarcely the words of an "unbridled voluptuary." No wonder that upon his return to Weimar he took up with the first comely girl that came his way, Christiane Vulpius, and that he defied scandal and isolation, seeing that the Duke, who had the shrewdest insight into his friend's total situation, stood by him. It remains on this score to be said that, before and after their legal alliance, Goethe was a faithful and affectionate husband to the ignorant girl he had taken into his house. He wrote immortal poems to other women. He always came home to Christiane as he had left her.

There is a third aspect of the Goethe legend which M. Valéry implied but did not define, namely, that Goethe was a pagan; that is to say, one supposes, in the modern sense of the word, an egoist, one who affirms the natural man, one who denies, as Nietzsche did, the values of the Judaeo-Christian moral tradition. That this notion could gain currency shows how ignorant the world has been of one of its loftiest spirits, despite the thousands of critical and scholarly volumes dedicated to his name. It is true that, except for a brief episode in his youth, Goethe had an intense aversion for dogmatic Christianity. He wrote at least one scurrilous epigram in which he ranged the symbol of the cross among the objects of his detestation. Nor, though he relished and admired it, did he share what he called his mother's Old Testamentary faith. But his active perception of the mystery of man and his world and of the need of grace to meet human aspiration—these were constant. In his twenty-eighth year he writes in his diary: "Took care of my bees and brought them to their winter rest. . . . What is man that Thou art mindful of him? And the son of man that Thou visitest him?" In preparation for his thirtieth birthday, he sets down a self-examination in the diary. It ends thus: "God help me to go on and give me more light, lest I stand so much in my own way." And some months later he writes in the diary: "I am gradually filled with great confidence. Please God that I may deserve it. I don't want what is easy, but what I truly desire . . . The best thing about me is that profound inner stillness in which I live and grow, despite the world."

These are not the only notes that are struck. Nor does he more than once make the observation: "I have been guilty of rather mad carryings-on on several occasions in my life. Don't think I didn't pay for them." The point is that the tenor and texture of Goethe's life, despite the wild hunting parties and drinking bouts in which he joined the Duke in the early Weimar years, were in accord with these severer aspects of his character. As he had, out of his then quite narrow means, supported his early friend, the dramatist Lenz, for a whole year, so in Weimar he gave an otherwise unknown protégé of his as much as one-third of his own meager salary. He sought wider privileges for a Jewish merchant; he wrote to Herder sharply concerning the care of the orphans of a subaltern army man:

"First they were in the orphanage where they were treated like swine; next they were in a boarding school, where they were treated like sheep. I want those boys to have a chance to become human." And this thread of active benevolence runs through his entire life, from his forty-day-long nursing of a disabled friend in Rome in 1787 to that handful of money he gave his physician in his seventy-seventh year, asking the latter to bestow it on one in need, neither the giver nor the receiver being known, and thus practicing, according to Maimonides, the highest type of human charity. Quite soberly, then, he was able to write to his son in 1816: "I have done a great deal for others in my life, perhaps more than was quite fair . . . You know enough of me to know that this is no idle boast."

He took, in the course of his life, sundry great liberties with the mere conventions, whether wisely or not, it is now futile to inquire. The steady tenor of his life was the reverse of pagan and may rather be summed up by an epigram he sent to Zelter in 1818:

> If I but knew the Eternal's way,
> Nothing could ever persuade me to stray;
> If the House of Truth had an open door,
> By God, I would leave it nevermore.

Or else it may be summed up by an entry in his diary of the year 1807: "The crucial thing is that a man be constantly reminded of the three necessary demands of the human spirit: God, immortality, virtue, and that these be guaranteed him as far as possible." And to this may be added the observation: "It is true that everything in nature is in flux, but behind this flux an eternal element is at rest." Within the moral life, according to Goethe, we are united to that element by love:

> Whatever as either truth or fable
> In myriad volumes thou hast spied,
> Is all but as a Tower of Babel
> Unless by love 'tis unified.

Metaphysically, if one likes, though Goethe disclaimed all formal philosophical skill or competence, man is allied to the Eternal by an identity according to some fashion:

> Did not the eye partake of sun,
> Sun would be darkness to our seeing;
> No splendor could from the divine be won
> Were God not part of mortal being.

Here and in many other passages the influence of Spinoza is evident enough. But that influence can easily be overemphasized, as Goethe did himself, partly because he loved Spinoza, the man; partly because what he held to be the Spinozistic view seemed to him to blend with his scientific insights, a little, finally, because he could use Spinoza as a weapon in his conflict with Christian doctrine.

The influence faded as the years went on. He came to very concrete conclusions. One was that "men are productive in poetry and art only so long as they have religious faith; after that all they produce are imitations and repetitions." He grounded and elaborated this conclusion in the notes to the *West-Eastern Divan*. Another conclusion to which he came was that the values of life, wherein lies its very meaning, can be validated only by the assurance of personal immortality:

> "You cling to immortality:
> Tell me why you refuse to doubt it?"
> Gladly! The chief ground is to me
> That we dare not to do without it.

This epigram may represent an hundred sayings in prose and verse, in familiar talk and in more formal expression. But the mood and temper out of which these convictions grew may be best illustrated by his young friend Sulpice Boisserée's account of the autumnal drive to Heidelberg on October 5, 1815. "The stars had risen. He spoke of his relation to Minna Herzlieb, the prototype of Ottilie; how he had loved her and how unhappy she had made him. Finally his speech became strangely mystical and prophetic. He would intersperse verses. At last, weary, irritated, half-mystic in mood, half-sleepy, we arrived in a sharp cold under a brilliant star-lit sky in Heidelberg."

Can anything be more *un*-pagan in tone, temper, atmosphere? He was aware of, nay, he summed up within himself all the eternal paradoxes of our mortal lot. "I extol the living spirit that for fiery death is fain," he had recently written. He was on his way to the quite ultimate conclusion:

> Unto God the Orient,
> Unto God the Occident;
> Northern lands and Southern lands
> Lie in the peace of His great hands.

[II]

It must be clear now that, contrary to legend and rumor, Goethe was neither libertine nor pagan. But it is necessary to go much farther. He did not at all belong to the *Aufklaerung*, the Age of Enlightenment, of "prose and reason," as Matthew Arnold called it, into which he was born. He was torn or tore himself out of the immediate context of history. In his youth, though he revered Lessing, the purest of the "enlighteners," he fled with Herder to the universal and magic sources of poetry. Yet in his later years he repudiated the Romantic movement, too, being prophetically aware of its falsely mystical tendencies and of the frenzied nationalism which was more and more to be its poisonous fruit.

His criticism of the Romantics, of their religion and their politics is well-known. His coolness to the nationalist uprising caused a grave enough scandal, that has been well remembered. What has not been emphasized is his unerring analysis of the Enlightenment, of that application of the mere reason toward the solution of

the "riddles of the painful earth," of which the bitter
dregs have not even yet been quite consumed. In 1784
manuscript copies of Voltaire's account of Frederick of
Prussia and himself were being passed around at the
Weimar court. Goethe wrote to Charlotte von Stein:
"You will find that he writes as though a god, say
Momus, that is, a god but a vulgarian, were to write
about a king . . . But that is indeed the character of
all of the productions of Voltaire's wit. There is no drop
of human blood; no spark of sympathy or human
warmth. There is an ease, an intellectual superiority, a
sureness of touch, which are enchanting. I say superiority, *not* elevation. He may be compared to a balloon
which, floating far above the earth sees plains below it,
where we see hills." "Superiority, *not* elevation"—is that
not the final word? But Goethe made direct and strong
attacks on the Enlightenment, even on its scientific
side, from the *Walpurgisnacht* of *Faust I*, in which the
phantasms and visions are declared to be impertinent,
seeing that the Enlightenment *had* taken place, to the
tremendous jibe of Mephistopheles in the second part
of the poem:

> 'Tis very like you learned gentlemen!
> What you can feel not is beyond your ken.
> What you can handle not is lost on you,
> And what eludes your fingers is not true.
> What you can weigh not simply has no weight,
> And coins not coined by you are counterfeit.

By the sheer power of his temperament, by unrivaled personal force, Goethe transcended both the age of prose and reason into which he was born and the age of romanticism and reaction in which his later years were passed. But—and this has not been remarked—he did take over from the eighteenth century certain elements of style, certain ways of expression which he transformed and transmuted for his personal uses, but which remained substructure and foundation even when he soared into regions of which the eighteenth century was unaware. He had the clarity and sententiousness, the terseness and balance, the epigrammatic edge and ultimate sobriety of speech which gave the eighteenth century its special distinction. Nor, as has often been supposed, are these qualities of style, these very antithetical sentence structures, of the order of a conscious artifice. We find them in the familiar letters of Voltaire, of Lessing, of Johnson. And they appear, transformed and transmuted by Goethe's transcendent use of them, even in the impassioned lyrics of the Strassburg period, even in "Welcome and Farewell," even in those incomparable lines to that tree into whose bark the lovers' names had been cut:

> Grow ever nearer heaven,
> O lofty tree, earth's pride.
> By raging storms unriven
> Thy sacred wood abide!
> Of graven names, O cherish
> The higher ones through time!

Well may the poet perish
Who wrought today this rime!

He could, of course, use the eighteenth-century style
on its own level, as in those almost unknown lines on a
reviewer, probably one of those reviewers of *Werther*
who, then as now, had no insight into the process by
which experience is transmuted into expression and how
thus art is forevermore divided from life.

A fellow came with me to dine.
Quite welcome he, to what was mine.
The menu was my ordinary.
The man devoured all he could carry
And for dessert cleaned out my store.
Scarcely that he could gorge no more
But to my neighbor does the devil
Take him to wag his tongue uncivil:
"Indifferently the soup was spiced,
The roast not crisp, the wine not iced."
The "so-and-so" I must aver.
'Twas a reviewer. Kill the cur!

The first step of a transmutation of that style, irrespective of time, is into that succinctness of lyric
elegance which we associate on the one hand with
Matthew Prior and, in another century, with Locker-
Lampson and Austin Dobson. A poem which illustrates
that method—also almost unknown, though Alfred de
Musset imitated it, not too happily—is "Self-Deception."

My lovely neighbor's curtains sway
And flutter up and down.

Doubtless she peers across the way
To see if I'm in town,

And if the sullen jealous mood
In which I turned on her
Still lingers, as I said it would,
Or ceased my heart to stir.

Alas, poor fool! Such thoughts as these
The lady would amaze.
I see it is the evening breeze
That in her curtain plays.

At his very highest, as in "Ultimate Aspiration" (*Selige Sehnsucht*), one of the topmost peaks of all poetry, there is but a glimmer left of that eighteenth-century shore. On the other hand, in a poem of the same great period (1815), the precise development of the image of the ripening and falling chestnut, the sententiousness, though with so lofty a lyric lift, the terseness and elegance once more betray the eighteenth-century stylistic foundation:

Let, dearest, a rewarding
Glance on those branches dwell,
The clustered fruits regarding
In their green, prickly shell.

For long no stirring eases
Their spheric quietude;
A bough tossed by the breezes
Rocks them in patient mood.

· 127 ·

Yet ever the brown kernel
Swells unto ripeness on,
To gain the air eternal
And to behold the sun.

At last the cleft shells alter
And give the cores release:
Thus do my lyrics falter
To thy beloved knees.

Nor did Goethe fail from time to time to return to the quite characteristic manner of the century that saw his birth. As late as 1820 he wrote fables in the tradition that runs from La Fontaine to Gay:

A little lake was bound by frost;
The frogs now at the bottom lost
Could neither croak nor swim nor spring,
But in their somnolence they swore:
If once again they reached the shore
They would the nightingales outsing.
The spring winds came, the ice thawed out,
The frogs landing with courage stout
Squatted complacent in the sun,
And croaked as they had always done.

Parallel with these returns to a stylistic foundation, the transformations of that style become ever more soaring:

What place thy friends may moulder,
Uncaring let it pass;
If under granite boulder,
If under wind-swept grass.

But while in life thou bidest,
See that, though dour the day,
For them thou still providest
What shall not know decay.

Here the transformation issues in the crystalline eternity
of the best things in the Greek Anthology. Yet under
our feet is still the green and friendly earth. But even
when Goethe quite "outsoars the shadow of our night,"
the precision and sententiousness, the clarity and order
of style remain:

In His name who, the self-created, spoke
The words eternal which the world evoke;
In His name Who Himself impregnates dust
With faith, love, power, activity and trust;
In His name Who, though often named He be,
Remains as essence still a mystery:
Far as thy hearing or thy sight may win
Thou findest but the known to him akin,
And though thy soul on fiery pinions rise
Image and simile must still suffice.
He draws thee on, impels thee forth to go,
And where thou treadest paths and places glow,
Numbers die to thee, time's an empty mood,
And every step measures infinitude.

The best place to study the foundations and transmuta-
tions of the Goethean style is, needless to say, *Faust*,
the poem of which the composition spanned sixty of
his eighty-two years. And here we may begin with certain famous quotations which have been for so long on

all lips because their searching insights are formulated with that eighteenth-century epigrammatic force. There is the universally known:

> Grau, teurer Freund, ist all Theorie
> Und gruen des Lebens goldner Baum.

> (Somber and gray, my friend, is theory,
> And green the golden tree of life.)

There is the tragically significant:

> Zwei Seelen wohnen ach in meiner Brust.
> (Two souls, alas, in my one bosom dwell.)

There is the deeply lyrical and pathetic:

> Ich bin zu alt um nur zu spielen,
> Zu jung um ohne Wunsch zu sein!

> (I am too old for mere distraction,
> Too young to be without desire!)

There is the matchlessly subtle and profound:

> So tauml' ich von Begierde zu Genuss,
> Und im Genuss verschmacht ich nach Begierde.

> (I stagger from desire to delight,
> And in delight am famished for desire.)

Numerous single verses, often culminating ones, have the contours of eighteenth-century prosody, recognizable despite the Goethean magic with which they are suffused. Such are:

Zu neuen Ufern lockt ein neuer Tag
(Unto new shores a day renewed persuades)

and

In Hoffnung reich, im Glauben fest.
(Wealthy in hope and firm in faith.)

It is to be emphasized that in the second part of
Faust this magic reaches a new level of continuous or
almost continuous intensity. It is true that the second
part has not the concrete earthy play of action and
passion which has made the first, chiefly at second or
third hand, even through the shallow music of Gounod,
one of the world's famous stories. But whenever, some-
times at long and dreary intervals, Goethe resumed
composition on the second part, something akin to
ecstasy came over him, the ecstasy of the seer. Meaning was drawn from that realm of "the Mothers"—that
core of things where destiny is created—and that meaning, apprehended in a state of ecstasy, produced the incomparable and untranslatable magic of form. Yet even
here the substructure of the eighteenth century is
visible in such a line of purest magic as

So schoen wie reizend, wie ersehnt so schoen

or the tremendous summing up of the fate of Paris:

Er folgte seiner Lust und Ilios fiel,

or that definition of one whole aspect of man's pathos:

Der Mensch ist ungleich, ungleich sind die Stunden

or in the less responsible loveliness of

>So wie sie wandeln machen sie Musik.

As the poem proceeds new forms arise from the groundwork. The forms are dazzling in variety and splendor.
Like fountains iridescent in the sunlight they leap
high in the songs of Euphorion, symbol of poetry in its
heavenward flight:

>Weiss ich nun wo ich bin!
>Mitten der Insel drin,
>Mitten in Pelops Land,
>Erde-wie seeverwand.

The fountains splash back into their basins—the tragic
iambics of the Attic stage, the heroic verses of neo-
classicism. Only in the fifth act does the pure ecstasy
prevail wholly. It culminates the first time in that song
of Lynkeus, the Watchman of the Tower, which is
Goethe's final confession and account of his own existence:

>Oh destined for seeing
>And stationed for sight,
>The tower is my being,
>The world my delight.

>My vision embraces
>The far and the near,
>Siderial spaces,
>The wood and the deer.

The grace of creation
My vigil did bless,
And in my elation
I pleased me no less.

Eyes happily ranging,
All that you have seen,
Though fortune was changing,
How fair it has been!

But of the general life of man this is not the last word. Hunger and Care and Guilt and Need hover about the aged Faust. In choral verse they proclaim his approaching end:

Es ziehen die Wolken, es schwinden die Sterne!
Dahinten, dahinten, von ferne, von ferne,
Da kommt er, der Bruder, da kommt er—der Tod.

But he, though stricken blind, though aware of death, defies the choral terrors and does not yield until his final beneficent deed and so his moral triumph have been proclaimed.

Yes, to this truth my heart is dedicated,
This last conclusion wisdom drew:
For him alone freedom and life fated
Who daily conquers them anew.
And though the sea still threatens, active here
Will men and children live their valiant year.
If such I could behold and be
With a free people on a soil as free—

Then to the moment transitory
"O fair one, linger," I could say,
Nor could the traces of my earthly story
Be by the aeons swept away.

In these famous verses we hear again the pulse beat of
the eighteenth century; we observe again, though lifted
to so transcendent a level, its sententiousness and precision. The final choruses of the redemption scene, as
those earlier Easter choruses in the first part of the
tragedy, doubtless owe rhythmic elements to the rimed
Latin hymns of the Medieval Church. Their music is
purer and more ardent; it is indeed, perhaps, the purest
and most ardent continuous verse music in all poetry.
But when a concrete meaning is to be formulated, as in
the passage which Goethe drew to Eckermann's special
attention, the old succinct and almost epigrammatic
note is once more, even though more faintly, heard:

Forever is from evil won
This scion of the spirit:
Who to the end strives nobly on
May our redemption merit.
And if the Love that is on high
Mark him from where its grace is,
The heavenly hosts toward him will fly
With welcome on their faces.

And Goethe also explained to Eckermann, at least by
implication, that he had here used the Christian "ma-
chinery," the content of which he had always so sharply

repudiated because, as he said: "We are not saved entirely through our own efforts but through the addition of Divine Grace." To this may be added the previous verses of the Pater Profundus:

> So ist es die allmaechtige Liebe,
> Die alles bildet, alles hegt.

> (And so it is the Love eternal
> Which forms and guards the universe.)

Now style and substance are inseparable, are one. Style *is* meaning and meaning, specific meaning, that which makes sense in the common phrase, can arise only from a universe—not from a multiverse—and from a universe, moreover, that is grasped by men, that makes sense to them. Faith and faith alone creates form. That is why *The Waste Land* of Eliot was deliberately a symbol of unfaith, and so of the death of meaning in a meaningless world; that is why both poetry and fiction are, *as* forms, which depend on meaning and on faith, in so desperate a state of crisis in this middle of the twentieth century. And of this situation of art Goethe was luminously aware and wrote in *Notes and Dissertations Toward a Better Understanding of the West-Eastern Divan* under the caption "Israel in the Desert," as follows: "All epochs in which faith reigns, irrespective of its form, are radiant, elevating and fruitful to themselves and posterity. All periods, on the other hand, in which unfaith, under whatever guise, attains a precarious victory, though they may boast a moment's specious glitter, fade from the recollection of posterity."

Goethe himself, however, lived in a world already devoid of coherent meaning and empty of faith. Great poetic forms were far to seek because there were no great and universal meanings. The process had begun in the early Renaissance and Shakespeare himself mirrors the formlessness and uncertainties of a breaking world. Now, in Goethe's own time, the use of the reason and that "true science" which according to Voltaire "necessarily leads to tolerance" and political liberation were being used to reconstitute an intelligible world. And Goethe, as we shall see, was averse from none of these ideals, assuredly not from those of science. But his vision went farther; it reached out for ultimates—for the ultimates of faith and form. And there was no form. All he had were the *forms* of the eighteenth century, the elegance, the succinctness, the balance and sobriety of the age of prose and reason. He used these, as has here been demonstrated. But for his vast lyrical productivity and for the 12,111 verses of *Faust* he needed great form, such as issues from great faith, from security within a universe known and understood. It was beyond his reach, as it is beyond our own. The last poet to have that completeness of great form arising from complete assurances of all meanings was Dante. Hence he could rise from hell to see the stars. "*E quindi uscimmo a riveder le stelle*"; hence he could let his poem culminate with the same word "stars" in a line that to him held the meaning of all meanings: *"L'amor chi muove il sol e l'altre stelle."* "The Love that moves the sun and all the stars."

Faust and the poems, as eternal as the *Divine Comedy,* and infinitely more significant to us, could not in a broken universe, have a form as tight, as complete, as impregnated with meaning, as Dante had. Yet Goethe did attain to a great form; he did transmute the eighteenth-century forms by virtue of meanings that he had found for himself, meanings which experience and observation, the poor and only resources of the modern artist, had furnished him. What were those meanings which he had wrung from his soul and from life? What were those meanings by the light of which the last supreme masterpiece of all literature, *Faust,* was wrought? It is clear how important such a question is to us. We face an utter despair in meaning and so an utter lack of form. We face *Finnegans Wake,* or, as a dim alternative, the neo-Catholicism which has enabled Mr. Eliot to write those "pastiches" of the Hebrew prophets, of Nehemiah and Ezekiel, which he calls *Choruses from 'The Rock.'* And even these are sociology rather than the exercise of the magic and creative word. Goethe and Goethe alone among the moderns wrested from life great meanings that issued in great unshattered forms. Let us see what those meanings were.

[III]

He found early in his life that power came from within. The continuous poetical excitement and productivity of his youth, not yet aware of grace, not yet knowing that *"alles ist wie geschenckt"*—all is as though given us—gave rise to those fragments of a Prometheus drama, of which one monologue soon became famous. That fame and influence Goethe lived in a measure to regret. He could see raw rebellious youth singed by a false Promethean flame. For himself, he gradually saw that the autonomy and freedom of the human personality resided in its real oneness and continuity. That oneness and continuity is the core of destiny.

> So must du sein, du kannst dir nicht entfliehn
> (Thus must thou be nor canst thyself escape.)

he wrote in the *Urworte*, the ultimate words. And earlier he summed the matter up: "A man may turn and twist as he will; he may undertake what he likes, he will always return to that path which nature originally assigned him." In the *Theory of Colors* he universalized this notion: "Every being that is conscious of its oneness seeks to maintain its proper situation unfragmentized and unmoved." In the *Elective Affinities*, amid many other amazing anticipations of the Freudian insights, he wrote: "What commonly happens to a man, repeats itself oftener than is thought, for his nature issues an immediate decision to this end." He was not averse in earlier days from the physiognomic studies of Lavater nor did he ever cease being fascinated by the relation of handwriting to character, though he warned repeatedly that the shadowy perceptions and analogies thus obtained be treated as poetry, as symbol, never as science, as fact. They were to him merely agreeable contributions to his assurance of the oneness, the preciousness, the persistence of human personality, of which he said that it carried the proof of immortality within itself. Perhaps the most trenchant maxim of this kind occurs in *Wilhelm Meister's Pilgrimage*, that late, inchoate, half-mystical work: "You can't get rid of what is truly yours, even were you to throw it away."

This unified and autonomous personality needed to be, nay, *was*, by its very character, a free, a self-sustaining one:

> In my saddle let me be the master!
> Hug your huts and tents against disaster!
> And in joy I'll ride to the horizon,
> Nothing but the stars to fix mine eyes on.

But it is neither the Fichtean subject which creates the world nor the arbitrary whimsical creature of later decadent cults. Its freedom is a freedom under the law of duty, under the eye of eternity. It is to be no sport of time or circumstance or wind of doctrine.

> Naught that is perishable
> Deem thou of worth!

> Us to eternalize
> Are we on earth.

And again: "We are on earth for the very purpose of rendering the perishable imperishable." Goethe was convinced that no opinion was valid which was not formed in the immediate consciousness of the historic millennia.

> Yield to the moment that arrives,
> When world and history are my station?
> Who in the ages sees and strives
> Alone can rise to speech and to creation.

Thus he defined or described the responsibilities of the free personality and, being attacked on many sides, applied it in a homely and familiar fashion to himself:

> If the Lord had wanted me to be
> Different, he would have seen to it.
> But since this talent he granted me,
> To trust me He thought fit.
> I've used it too freely to reckon,
> Nor know the final score;
> When it serves no more,
> Be sure He'll beckon.

This application to himself he was quite willing to universalize. "So divinely is the world ordered that each one in his right situation, place and time balances all else." But his final demand of the free personality was stern and exacting:

The strict original mind
Never abandon!
Ground that the mob picks blind
Is plain to stand on.
The highest reason use
And be its warder;
The lore that sages choose
Is always harder.

And the deepest and all-inclusive statement of the matter, of that immortal worth of the free personality, irrespective of good or evil fortune, is in the *West-Eastern Divan*:

Folk and clown and conqueror seeking
This, confess it so to be:
Crown and core of mortal being
Is man's personality.

Ways of life need little choosing
If the self itself sustains;
Winning is not more than losing
If what one is—one remains.

This free personality is the object of grace; it is the source of vision and of art. "Poetic content is the content of one's own life." To which may be added the most famous of Goethe's sayings on this matter: "Whatever of mine has become known represents only the fragments of a long confession." And, as several critics, among them Thomas Mann, have pointed out, this autobiographical impulse, when it issues in plastic creation, is inseparable from the pedagogical or, at least, from the other-regarding impulse. The artist transmutes his experience into expression in order that others may live and express themselves vicariously and thus understand and experience more luminously their mortal lot. Therefore Goethe spoke a literal truth when he said: "Even at our moments of highest happiness and deepest distress we have need of the artist."

This modern artist personality, self-appointed and originally self-created, prevails through the weight of the character from which experience and its transmutation into art arise. Goethe once wrote to Schiller: "The best thing about a good artist is that he has nothing to lose if truth turns out to be true. So many men fight genius and veracity for the single reason, that they would be destroyed if they had to admit its existence." And earlier he wrote him: "What we must do under all circumstances is to forget this age in which we live, and work exclusively according to our own convictions." This stringent austerity and obedience to a law of one's own choosing and creation does not exclude a right to humility.

> The masters' works I look upon
> And clearly see what they have done.
> I look at my own stuff—a thing or two,
> And see what I should have tried to do.

And indeed on this point he could be charmingly natural and human, as when he wrote to a friendly critic: "The world does its best to make us indifferent to praise or blame. But this does not succeed, so that whenever we hear favorable judgments of ourselves and such as coincide with our own convictions, we are only too pleased to exchange resignation for relish."

The action of grace on the free creative personality argues its oneness with the nature of the universe. "Goethe confessed," his young friend Boisserée wrote, "that his poems came suddenly into his mind in their entirety, whenever they are right. Then he has to record them immediately, otherwise they are irrecoverable." But grace can be met or prepared for by discipline. "No work of genius," Goethe wrote to Schiller, "can be improved or freed of its faults by taking thought or by the consequence of taking thought. What genius can do is to raise itself by both reflection and action to a level upon which it at last produces faultless work." The artist, in other words, is the symbol of man, of the eternal Faustian personality, who errs, who strives, who experiences, who transmutes his experience into an act under the consenting grace of God.

Now this free personality, this immortal soul, whether artist or not, lives in society. And it is Goethe's relations to society and to its organization that have had, ever since the days of Boerne and Heine and the Young Germany Movement, a rather sinister effect on his fame. Not only was he for a number of years the ranking minister of an autocratically though humanely governed Duchy; he was guilty of a few—a very few— outrageous outbursts of prejudice. These outbursts have been emphasized by so-called liberals ever since. When their context is examined, however, it is quite clear that they were what is now loosely called temperamental, due to frustration in love—and Goethe was generally frustrated—or else due to the state of the barometer, from which he suffered intensely. He wrote to Schiller in 1803: "In December I always understand so well how Henri III ordered the execution of the Duke of Guise, just because the weather got on his nerves. At this moment I envy Herder on hearing that he is about to be buried." It is unwise—so much is clear—to let his moments of human weakness obscure his immensely cogent criticism of the social and political trends which arose in his day and in which we are still so deeply implicated.

Let us begin with his earliest completely formulated reaction to the French Revolution. It constitutes one of the "Venetian Epigrams."

> Of France's ill fate let the great beware,
> But let the humble have an equal care!
> Yes, the great fell. But who protects the mass
> Against the mass, which its own tyrant was?

We know a great deal more about revolutions than Goethe did; we are still forced to ask the crucial question that he put. The years passed. Napoleon, the heir of the revolution, conquered Europe. Goethe did not see the vulgarian in Napoleon and had a weakness for him, fed by Napoleon's compliments to himself. He was cool to the German national uprising against the conqueror and was therefore quite open-eyed to the quality of the reaction after Waterloo. So he wrote in December 1815:

> Thank God for all our benefits!
> On Helena the tyrant sits!
> But while the single one was banished
> Our hundred tyrants have not vanished
> Who forge, to cut our peace in two
> A Continental system new.
> Germany's to be isolated,
> A *cordon sanitaire* instated,
> That in our pure midst be not heard
> Least echo of a foreign word;
> While on our laurels we repose
> And look no farther than our nose.

Is it any wonder that the Nazis detested and repudiated him and found that he was far too dark for a true "Aryan" and cast a fantastic doubt on the name of Lindheimer, borne by his maternal grandmother? But equally fantastic was the Soviet participation in the bicentennial commemoration. For he had no illusions about mass actions and mass decisions. "Each one wants to be master and none is lord of himself," he said in one form or another again and again. As for the majority! "It consists of a few vigorous shock troopers, of rogues who see their profit in agreement, of weaklings who adapt themselves and of a great multitude that rolls along without in the least knowing what it wants."

And therefore he knew and declared that "everything that is great and wise is confined to a minority." And he was so sure of his ground because, in full possession of the past and its teachings, he saw with prophetic exactness the turn that history was taking. "New inventions can and will be made, but nothing new is left to be discovered concerning man's moral nature." The ultimate had been discovered long ago. He was himself to formulate it thereafter in the seven plain words to which one must always return: *"Wer Gutes will, der sei erst gut."*

It was not that he did not understand revolution. Very early he had written: "Inappropriate laws and penalties provoke the evil." Like Thoreau—the comparison is astonishing but exact—he wanted governments to be humbler and more scrupulous. "Revolutions," he said to Eckermann, "are quite impossible if governments are steadily just and steadily aware and meet the necessity of timely improvements without resisting them so long that amelioration must be wrung from them by the people." And again he said: "I hate violent overthrow because it always involves the destruction of good, whatever be its gain. I hate those who bring it about and equally those who made it inevitable." He knew no less all the ultimate, the metaphysical difficulties. "He who acts is always devoid of conscience; conscience belongs to the contemplative man alone." But his shrewdness never missed the concrete facts of life. "There is no such thing as patriotic art and patriotic science." And the corollary? "The more evil a land, the hotter are its patriots." And as a scientist, finally, he defined the whole matter of our time at its deepest level. "This modern period has too high an opinion of itself by reason of the great mass of material which it contains. But man's advantage consists solely in the measure in which he can treat and become master of that material." He had no trust in the mere devices of men still unredeemed, none in their sudden hot and cruel utopian plans. He spoke of himself at the end of his life as a liberal. He did so with a good conscience. Such a one, he said, "is contented in this imperfect world with the good until time and circumstance favor the creation of something better."

Goethe's views of the centrality of the autonomous personality, its necessary persistence, its creative activity, whether in art or life, were built upon an unshakable foundation. He was no systematic thinker. He was sage and poet and might well have repudiated any statement of the intercoherence of his vision of the sum of things. But that intercoherence exists and is most precious to us. For it illuminates the heresies that threaten to destroy our civilization. Among these are the overemphasis on environmental forces and a brutal insistence on false universals to which men are made to conform or perish. The old barbaric alternative of Islam —the Koran or the sword—is in high and bloody fashion. Calmly the great Goethean voice comes to us across the years: "At all times it was individuals who strove after knowledge, never the period. It was the period which gave Socrates the hemlock and burned Huss at the stake. The periods have always been alike." It is the spirit alone—*der Geist*—which is "autochthonous." The interpenetration of nature with spirit, of *Natur* with *Geist* —this it is that makes man human. "The ability to elevate the sensual, to vivify the most torpid matter by drenching it with mind—such is the surest proof of man's divine origin." This cannot be done with universals. It must be done with concrete things. But things are more than things. Only from concrete things do universals arise. But not in the mere manner of the sciences of classification. "This is true symbolism, that the specific represents the general, not as dream or shadow, but as instant and immediate revelation of the unfathomable." Or, in another formulation: "Every existing thing is the analogue of all existence; it is for this reason that all being strikes us as discrete and interwoven at the same time." Or, once more: "All that takes place is a symbol and by representing itself perfectly it contains the significance of all else." The all but last line of Faust, of course, says that, too. "*Alles Vergaengliche ist nur ein Gleichness!*" "All that is perishable is but similitude." And the average amorphous man resists this cognition. "Most men are themselves formless. They can give themselves and their being no form (*Gestalt*). Hence they seek to rob objects of their form (*Gestalt*) in order that substance may become loose and amorphous like themselves."

Need it be added that he insisted: "Humanity? That is a mere abstraction. From of old there have existed only individuals and for all time there will be only such."

The exemplary human being is the poet, the creator. As he lives from within outward, as he carries within himself the whole world by anticipation, so do, so may, all men. And the poetic, the creative process, is the analogue of all the processes of the human spirit. Here is the central and crucial and universally applicable *locus classicus:* "This is the great difference, whether the poet seeks the particular in order to illustrate the general or whether he seeks the general within the particular. The former leads to allegory. . . . The latter method constitutes the true method of poetry which expresses the particular without thinking of the general or even pointing it out. He who grasps the particular in vivid fashion is given the general, whether he is aware of it or becomes aware only late." This passage is quite late and occurs in a reminiscent account of his own and Schiller's creative procedures. But long, long years before, he had immortally summed up the whole matter in the poet's defense of himself in the Prologue on the Stage to the first part of *Faust.*

When Nature the unending thread devises,
Upon indifferent whirling spools to spin,
When from all creatures' clashing mass arises
A sullen and discordant din—
Who cleaves the dull monotonous gyration
And into living rhythms divides the whole,

· 149 ·

Who calls the singular to general consecration
Wherein the chords accordant nobly roll,
Who shapes the storm as symbol of our passion,
In thoughtful souls lets sunset glow be red,
Who rifles all the floral spring to fashion
A path for the beloved's tread,
Who plucks the green leaves without form or meaning
To be as crowns of human honor sealed,
Unites the gods from safe Olympus leaning?—
Man's power in the poet's soul revealed.

Man's power is best revealed in the poet's soul. But it is man's; it is his own. The autochthonous, immortal human personality stands at the core and center of the world and re-creates it in its own image. It "calls the singular to general consecration" and so makes music of discordance and a divine world out of the materials of nature.

It may not be inapposite to end this discourse, as it was begun, with a quotation from the late Paul Valéry. Horrified in 1934 by the clearer and clearer development of National Socialism in Germany, instantly aware of its complete analogy to Soviet theory and practice, he spoke in deep dismay to a group of French collegians. "Our generation is seeing in these brief years the idea of man pass from that supreme preciousness wrought by so many generations to a totally different image of him. Henceforth man is being conceived by many as having worth only as an element in a social system, living only by it and for it; he is but a means within the collective life; all separate value is refused him, for he can receive nothing save from the community and has no gifts to give except to it." Rightly Valéry derived from this blasphemous and execrable heresy the death of all moral values; rightly he asked whether this was not "training and fashioning man" as animals are trained in a circus; eloquently he stigmatized the false and shallow universalism of an epoch "whose sole law seems to be to carry the intermixture of all things to some extremity of confusion, incoherence, and intimate irritation."

Whence do these horrors and miseries derive? Ultimately in part, at least, from a crude, pagan acceptance of nature and a servile identification of man with nature, as an outworn, materialistic science chose to delineate it. Thence arose the dreadful doctrine of an uncritical adaptation to environment, of subservience to the machine and to that brutal figment called "social forces." Is it not then exact to say that of all modern voices that of Goethe is most sorely needed—that tranquil, penetrating imperishable voice which bids the free personality reshape nature in its own image, suffuse nature with values derived from a source beyond itself and to transcend the natural by man's two sovereign gifts: the gift of goodness, the gift of the pursuit of perfection.